CW00920101

First published in
This edition p
BACKPAGE

www.backpagepress.co.uk
@BackPagePress

ISBN: 9781909430341
eBook ISBN: 9781909430358

A catalogue record for this book is available
on request from the British Library

Typeset by BackPage
Cover design by Polaris Publishing Ltd
Front cover images: Getty images and Shutterstock
Back cover images: Bradley Ormesher
Printed in Great Britain by MBM Print

To Dad

You passed on a love of football

and, even better, a love of words

CONTENTS

INTRODUCTION

Hello and *dobro pozhalovat* (Добро пожаловать). Now, I'm not going to lie. When I left for the World Cup in Russia it was with one, big target in mind. July 16. That was the day after the final when I'd be boarding a flight at Moscow Sheremetyevo and going home again.

I'm not one of those journalists who the job has made jaded, but I couldn't help feeling weary about the finals. 2017-18 had been another long season and I have two half crazy and completely beautiful little daughters I don't see enough of. My main thought was getting the work done and beating that retreat from Moscow, going home to Leicester, then on holiday.

I flew to Russia, first stop St Petersburg, on June 12 and a couple of days before that, had a pint with a mate, Matt. All I did was complain. Complain about time away from the family. Complain about being on an organised 'school trip' with other journalists. Complain that tournaments were never any good any more. And complain, most of all, about Russia. I'd just been to the News UK headquarters in London for a security briefing given to *Times*, *Sunday Times* and *Sun* reporters travelling to the finals. It had been a long, grim lecture about cyber security, personal safety, logistics nightmares, Russian state-sponsored violence and Vladimir Putin.

Our security people issued us new laptops, mobiles and SIM cards, in case of hacking, and special locking devices to attach to our hotel room doors to guard against break-ins. They told us to put tape over the camera eyes on our smartphones in case the Russians found a way to tamper with the devices and use them to spy on us.

I didn't buy all of it, but I did get the gist. Russia = bad. So that was one reason my cup of World Cup enthusiasm was hardly overflowing. Another came from my experience of recent finals. In 2014 it had been wonderful being in Brazil, but the actual football there was flat and anticlimactic. Same with South Africa in 2010. The 2006 World Cup in Germany was slightly better, but only slightly, while the quality of the 2002 edition could be summed up by the teams finishing third and fourth: Turkey and South Korea.

Throw in a sequence of underwhelming European Championships and I reckoned I hadn't seen a really good tournament in as much as 20 years. There seemed no reason why Russia would be any different, and there were the fears about hooliganism and potential VAR glitches to throw in.

I also had low expectations about my brief, which was to stay close to and focus on England. Can you blame me? England's tournament campaigns since 2004 had trodden the same tired path of hope, hype, then mishap. I hadn't seen them truly play well in a tournament match since a young Wayne Rooney was rampant at the Euros in Portugal, 14 years ago. As a Scot, I was at least spared emotional involvement in England's failures. But as a journalist, I'd long grown to feel I was reporting on a story that had got stale. At least in their last two finals England found ways of messing up that were so spectacularly humiliating there was a certain scope when writing about them, but how could they top going out to Iceland at Euro 2016? Lose to some actual whales and volcanoes?

Not that another England calamity was my expectation. They were patently better under Gareth Southgate. They had become a more intelligent and unified team, playing football more in step with the rest of the world, so what I thought they'd achieve in Russia was competency. But competency doesn't grab headlines, does it? Let alone fill 1500-word broadsheet think pieces.

My final fear was boredom. As a Sunday reporter, who publishes once a week, tournaments can be a challenge. They're not like the regular season, where you spend the days when you're not live and on deadline travelling around, doing interviews, meeting contacts and going to events and press briefings. My remedy in previous tournaments had been to get out and about and see as many matches and training camps as possible, but a combination of England's schedule and the cost of Russian travel would ensure I couldn't do this. How was I going to fill my time?

The blog that became this book was born out of all these worries. Something to help the time pass. Something to make a trying assignment more fun. I toyed with a few ideas. A podcast? I don't quite have the chutzpah. Start work on a book I'm planning? It wasn't quite the right time. I settled for something simple: a daily update for those who follow my journalist Facebook page. I thought I could try predicting the scores of upcoming games and pick out different players to watch. It would be a diversion and a way of keeping engaged with the wider tournament beyond just England. When I sat down to write the first entry, on June 13, I realised I needed a few remarks to introduce what I was going to do, and that's all the first update was: a few throwaway paragraphs, some notes about the tournament to come.

The next day, the day of Russia v Saudi Arabia in the opening game, I began with the predictions and players, and wrote some more preamble – again, throwaway stuff. The shift came the following afternoon when, at the England Media Centre, I found myself playing darts with Dele Alli. Now that was something to tell people about. It was unexpected, unusual, and gave me a small but special insight into one of the world's most valuable young players.

Those elements I've just described struck me as exactly what I should be relaying to readers in my reports home from Russia. But an oche face-off with Dele Alli? A little too whimsical and personal for an article in *The Sunday Times*. Having a blog on the go was perfect. It was the right space for 'Darts with Dele,' my Day 4 missive, and the wonders of digital meant I could post pictures and a video, too.

And so it went. I quickly realised there were many more things that I wanted to communicate from Russia, which did not quite fit in *The Sunday Times*, but were ideal for the more dressed-down milieu of a Facebook blog. Some were things that just happened, socially or in the course of reporting; some were thoughts about the football that popped into my mind, and I made the discovery that there was a lot of stuff, actually, that I had wanted to discuss for years.

This was largely stuff about journalism and the particular job we do, and lives we lead, as football reporters. I love my trade and the little corner of it we sports writers are privileged to inhabit. But it can be a challenging existence. My entries about journalism were part therapy and part celebration, looking back. In truth, the score predictions and players-to-watch bits became afterthoughts. Writing the preambles was what I looked forward to. I loved the responses readers posted on my page and the experience of being off-the-cuff and direct. When you write for a newspaper, you try to be exact and polished and weigh your words. Social media? The beauty is being instant, conversational.

I didn't overthink it. Whenever I knew I had an hour to spare, whether on a plane or in a hotel breakfast room or media centre, I opened up the laptop and just typed. Often, I already had an idea what I was going to write about, but not always. Sometimes I just picked a starting point and let the rest follow – an example was Day 13 and the email about Victoria Lopyreva that sparked the entry 'Models and Messi'.

Over 33 days, the blog ran to around 40,000 words. Had any editor asked me to produce 40,000 words in addition to all the stuff I was doing for *The Sunday Times* and *Times*, I'd have been on to HR. But the blog didn't feel like extra work. It was pleasure. It felt like my own little space within the tournament and one of the bits of my day to which I most looked forward.

Day 18, 'Personal Connections', gave me the opportunity to explain something about football journalism, and the angles that I'm coming from, that in the spirit of full disclosure I had always wanted readers to know. Day 20, 'England', was another chance to be personal about subjects that, because of family history, feel like they've run through my life – identity and nationality. It was also an excuse to soak in a bath in a Moscow hotel re-watching 'The Impossible Job' into the early hours. And who wouldn't want to do that?

Day 23, 'Potemkin Nation', allowed me to explore history and geopolitics in ways football hacks normally don't get to. Day 32, 'The Final Jamjar', was the last of several entries where I indulged my statto side. Day 30, 'Beating the Bridges', was really just the chance to tell the story of a great night out – and great nights out have been the stuff of journalism probably since the guys on *Acta Diurna,* the world's first newspaper, started getting out and about looking for stories in Ancient Rome.

It made all the difference that my fears about the tournament, not to mention Russia itself, were unfounded. Russia was a revelation and the football was an even nicer surprise. In the club game this is an era where positive, intelligent and technical teams hold sway and the same vibe was carried onto the international stage. Russia 2018 had more goals, better matches, and more consistently open and entertaining play than any World Cup since the first I reported on, France 1998.

England helped, too. Reporting on them was far from the chore I had anticipated. Indeed for a Scotsman, those Three Lions became dangerously cuddly and endearing at times. Southgate brought a thoughtfulness to the task of leading his country that put current politicians, never mind previous managers, to shame. It was a pleasure watching young, un-starry and light-on-ego players, like Harry Maguire and Jordan Pickford, grow. It was great watching an England squad with humility and no little talent making the most of themselves rather than the least.

Reaching a semi-final was something of which I felt England were capable, right from the start (see Day 1: Back of the Nyet). But if it was to happen, I didn't expect the journey to grip people back home in quite such a way. Sadly, I didn't have the foresight to buy shares in waistcoat manufacturers, or select Kieran Trippier as one of my 'World Cup stars to watch' back on June 12. But

England's success gave impetus to the blog: there's nothing like writing for an audience that's excited and engaged.

As I posted more entries, a few people said I should turn the blog into a book, so in the spirit in which the blog began, a spirit of just throwing stuff out there, here goes...

A last element, or rather person, to mention: Mrs Northcroft, my better half, Jan. In that security briefing they instructed us to stay off social media, for fear of hackers and identity theft, and so those 40,000 words that went up on Facebook? None were actually posted by me. For I wasn't on Facebook. Back home in Leicester, Jan was. I'd write a blog entry, then email it to her and WhatsApp some photos or video, and she'd log in as me and create the post.

Often, my material arrived when she was in a playpark with our little one, Cora, or just about to do the school run to collect our eldest, Ishbel. Once, the stuff arrived when she was at an Eid-come-children's-birthday party, another time when she was setting off for the school fete. Somehow, via the powers of multi-tasking that lie beyond men, she was always able to collate, edit, and get the stuff up online almost straight away. She also managed and responded to the comments on my behalf.

So, Jan was actually my star of the World Cup. But Mbappe, Pogba, Kante, Griezmann; Modric, Perisic, Rakitic, Subasic; Southgate, Stones, Maguire, Trippier; Hazard, Mina, Golovin, Inui; Lagavulin, Nizhny Novgorod and St Petersburg: they proved pretty stellar, too. My love for tournaments has been rekindled.

Hope you enjoyed it as well. Hope you enjoy this. In the end, July 16 came round too soon. Since, the strangest thing has been happening. I'm even looking forward to Qatar.

— Day One, June 14, 2018

Back of the Nyet

Greetings from Russia and from Repino – accurately described by Paul Hayward, chief sports writer of *The Daily Telegraph*, as Formby-on-the-Gulf-of-Finland. I'm here near England's training base, on the sleepy coastline north of St Petersburg, and thought I'd post a few bulletins to pass the time. I also felt like titling the first one with a shabby pun – apologies for that.

In just two days' time another World Cup kicks off, so first things first: who'll do well? Before yesterday I felt Spain were being underestimated to such an extent they were almost getting to be dark horses. Many people were placing them "among the favourites" but very, very few were tipping them to go close to winning. I thought that strange. Spain have the best keeper, perhaps the best centre-back pairing, the best possession game, great attacking full-backs and an array of penetrative and creative players, starting with Andres Iniesta and extending to David Silva, Isco, Marco Asensio and Thiago Alcantara. Plus Diego Costa up front. Plus one of my favourite young talents in the world game, Saul Niguez.

But Julen Lopetegui's sacking throws everything in doubt. The news broke when we were on a press shuttle bus on the way to England training and it had a WTF impact that breaking news very seldom has on hardened journalists. We've all seen a lot at tournaments (not least thanks to England's soap operas and mishaps down the years) but sacking your manager 48 hours before an opening game? Not even the FA have ever done that.

And yet it kind of tickles me that the World Cup has just

been heftily impacted by a guy who once played at Ross County for Hamilton Accies in the Scottish League Cup: Luis Rubiales, the Spanish Federation boss whose decision it was to fire Lopetegui and replace him with Fernando Hierro. I'm also nursing a little fantasy that Hierro, remembering his debt to Bolton Wanderers, is going to install Ivan Campo as his No.2.

Before the change, my tip was for Spain to reach the final – but lose to Brazil – and I still think this can happen if Hierro proves a Zidane-style appointment. Zidane-style in the sense of being a galvanising figure to a group of star players via his own charisma and iconic status, more than any coaching or tactical impetus.

Brazil? Just a beautifully balanced side. They can counter, can play possession. Goals in plenty areas, steel where they need it. Energy. Mentality. And in Neymar that extra element of quality and inspiration. Basically, with World Cups, whenever Brazil get it right they tend to win – and under Tite they look to be getting it right.

I feel Germany are over-rated (feel free to throw this one back at me when the old *Mannschaft* go all the way to Moscow). Why? Their best players – except Toni Kroos – aren't quite what they were (Thomas Muller, Mesut Ozil, Sami Khedira, Manuel Neuer). They miss the on/off pitch influence of Philipp Lahm and Bastian Schweinsteiger, the two leaders of the team in 2014. Their youngsters aren't quite there yet. And they've left their best one – Leroy Sane – at home.

France? Not as good in reality as on paper. Paul Pogba, Ousmane Dembele, Kylian Mbappe, Hugo Lloris, Olivier Giroud ... none had stellar seasons. The great wee N'Golo Kante is still there and I like the look of their defence, but I'm not sure about Didier Deschamps. Do France have the coach, the personality and the form to do their billing of favourites – in the eyes of many – justice?

England? It would not surprise me that much if they reached the semi-finals, but equally I wouldn't be shocked if they went out in the group stage. Tunisia is a tricky opening game. They are a competitive, organised side with a fairly youthful feel – a lot of players French-born or playing in France. They'll be like good mid-table Premier League opposition and my worry about England is they don't hurt teams enough. They control games, space, the ball, better than England sides have done in a long time. But they don't make periods of good play tell. They don't score as many goals as they should. If they're a bit off against Tunisia it could well be a draw, which would put them in a slightly precarious position. But if I was putting money on it, England will have a decent tournament and get to the last eight and everyone will go home happy with the progress made and the positive vibe struck by a very likeable young squad and manager.

Shocks? I fancy Morocco to do something in that 'group of death' and perhaps finish ahead of a weary Portugal. Egypt can have a run if Salah is playing at anything like his best. Expect Senegal to be well worth watching. Denmark, Uruguay, Serbia, Peru are intriguing outsiders.

What else? I fear racism and VAR problems and FIFA not dealing well with either. I hope, and think, the hooligan threat might not materialise. From what I've seen so far (and it's only a very small snapshot), Russia is going to put on its best face and host an orderly tournament, as nearly always happens with World Cups. You shouldn't judge a country by its leader and the Russians I've encountered so far have been friendly and humorous. I was in St Petersburg last night for my birthday and wow, what a city. It is a shame so many fans have been put off coming.

Prediction today: Russia 1 Saudi Arabia 1

Player to watch: Aleksandr Golovin. I'm told that the *Gazzetta Dello Sport* story of yesterday is true and that Juventus have bid for him, a low opening offer likely to rise. It's no wonder, he's some prospect

What happened next: The hosts defied expectations by running out 5-0 winners, with Golovin scoring the fifth. He signed for Monaco from CSKA Moscow on a five-year deal after the World Cup

— Day Two, June 15

Meegyets and Managers

Привéт

That, of course, means 'hello' in Russian. According to Google Translate. *Preevyet.*

All is good in Repino, except it rivals the Highlands of Scotland for midges. Or *meegyets* as I'd imagine the locals call them. Press-wise, things are starting to get a bit more serious here, with all the "what a lovely bunch of boys" stuff written about the England squad in the build-up giving way to harder reporting. Some of the lads from the daily papers appear to have found out Gareth Southgate's intended starting XI for the Tunisia game: Ashley Young instead of Danny Rose, a mistake in my opinion (if you play wing-backs you're pinning your plans on width – you *have* to play a left footer on the left, so he can go outside). It will be interesting to see if these stories start to change the so-far-happy dynamic between the FA, the England team and us. Traditionally, the FA and the England manager have always hated team info leaking out. Gareth is different in many ways, mind you.

Russia 5 Saudi Arabia 0
(and what makes a good international manager)

By the end, I was loving that opening game. The old cliché about how it is "always good for the tournament when the hosts start well" is actually true. It has an effect on locals, the country's authorities, their press – all of that. And it was also just great to see some goals and a bit of artistry in a fixture that had looked pretty grey on paper. Golovin was wonderful and showed how clever Juventus were for getting in there first. Not that Russia themselves were that great. I've just been diagnosed with a badly arthritic knee, but I could still beat Sergei Ignashevich in a race. Hopping. And even though he scored twice, admittedly with great finishes, I thought Denis Cheryshev was ordinary on the ball in central midfield and his partner, Roman Zobnin, was even ordinary-er.

Saudi Arabia were a bit pathetic. A few reports this morning are describing them as "no-hopers" and "useless" but I'm not sure that's right. To me, they looked quite accomplished technically. Their problem was mentality and organisation. They played about 15 yards too deep, doggedly kept trying to play out from the back even though Russia's main ploy was a fierce high press, and they were so meek and timid in everything they did: tackling, passing, shooting. It made me look at their bench and Juan Antonio Pizzi: appointed in November as the Saudis' third coach in three months, and a guy who had somehow failed to take Chile – South American champions, Alexis Sanchez and Arturo Vidal et al – to these finals.

Pizzi was specifically brought in for the tournament because his previous career high, which was winning a drab 2016 Copa America with Chile, was seen as making him something of a tournament specialist. Hmm. At least the Saudis were trying to think of tournament and international football as something separate and special compared to the club game. They tried for a manager they thought would excel in that specific arena.

I've long felt that is the way to go. International management and club management require quite different skills. In international management certain things become far more important than in the club game, and certain things far less so. For example: dealing with the media, clarity of decisions, simple messages, personal charisma, being able to set a 'tone' or 'culture'; these are very important at international level. Training-ground brilliance, complex tactical ideas? Less so, because there is far less scope and time to bring such things to bear.

For example, David Moyes said to me last week he'll be interested to see how many teams at the World Cup use a pressing game. It's the rage in club football, but good pressing requires a significant amount of co-ordination and rehearsal. Get a pressing game wrong and you're in big trouble. In the World Cup you might see relatively little of it. Sitting back before counter-attacking is much easier to coach.

Today's games are interesting in terms of the managers. Spain of course have Hierro in charge now, and he has limited and fairly moderate club experience. One so-so season with Oviedo. But what he does have is charisma, confidence and an instant cause to fire his players – 'let's put things right for the nation after Lopetegui's treachery'. So he actually has the dynamics, as an international boss, to do quite well.

Portugal have wily old Fernando Santos, whose long career in club management was average, but who has found a niche in the international game, first with Greece then with his own country. Similarly, Carlos Queiroz, Iran's best-ever manager, is someone who thrives as an international boss, but has been less successful club-wise.

Joachim Low may be the ultimate example of this and it bodes well for Gareth Southgate. He was dealt a very difficult hand and treated badly by Middlesbrough after doing a decent job there, and I think the international scene really suits him. It's his intelligence, the quality of his personal dealings and the respect he commands from others in his quiet, upstanding manner. He's the Head Boy who the lads like, too. And, quietly, Southgate makes very strong, brave and clear decisions.

On the other end of the spectrum, in today's games we also have Hector Cuper in charge of Egypt. Cuper had such a good club career but will his caution and dourness inhibit what could be a team inspired by Salah?

Predictions today: Egypt 0 Uruguay 1; Morocco 1 Iran 0; Spain 3 Portugal 1

Player to watch: Hakim Ziyech, Morocco. I fancy Morocco as dark horses in this tournament and Ziyech is their player with that bit of flair and devilment. He stood out for Ajax in their 2017 Europa League run and Premier League clubs will be watching how he gets on in Russia

What happened next: Uruguay did indeed win by the only goal – but Iran upset Morocco 1-0. Spain and Portugal shared six goals in an all-time classic. Ziyech remains at Ajax – where he continues to dazzle

— Day Three, June 16

Whatever Happened to that Ronaldo kid?

Just a short one because Saturday is deadlines-day for a Sunday hack ... but, wow, Spain v Portugal! I'd go as far as to say that was the best World Cup game I've seen in 20 years. Think back over all the World Cups since 1998 and there aren't many matches that stand out like that one.

I interviewed Ronaldo one-on-one, just the once. It was in 2005 and I was a contributor to a £3000 luxury book commissioned on Manchester United. For the book I did sit-downs with Rooney, Giggs, Solskjaer, Van Nistelrooy and Schmeichel ... but Ronny was different. Our slot was an hour. After about 20 minutes he started looking at his enormous, bejewelled watch, and began disengaging. This was in contrast to the other players, who were focused and up for it, in that 'can-do' way of players in the Alex Ferguson era when they were on club duty.

Ronaldo was having a difficult season and the wow-factor of his early United career seemed to be ebbing. I and the other writers working on the book had to compile a list of the top 50 players in United's history. I think we put Ron at No.31 or something, below Nicky Butt. The sense was that he was a wonderful talent who might just never realise his potential (a bit like how his great friend, Ricardo Quaresma, turned out). I've made a few very bad predictions in my journalistic career, but this has to be the very worst.

The thing about Ronaldo at that age (despite his boredom at my questions) was that he was a really nice kid, beneath the ego-driven exterior. The senior players at United were quite hard on him – but they loved him, too.

Fergie was the same. Underpinning his extraordinary career is a certain humility: he doesn't take his talent or profession for granted; he works and works and works at maintenance and improvement.

I loved watching Spain last night. The quality of their touches and movement was way higher than anything we've seen in the competition so far, and perhaps are likely to see (especially Isco and David Silva), but good as they were, they almost lost to a B-grade team powered by one absolutely incredible footballer. That is the power of Ronaldo. 84 international goals by the way. 84!!!

On Spain: signs that Pique, Busquets and Iniesta aren't quite what they were. But, Isco and Silva apart, Ramos, Alba and of course Costa were fantastic. David De Gea? Like a Sefton Park Cricket Club Sunday XI fine leg when trying to field that Ronaldo shot. What came over him?

Predictions today: France 4 Australia 0; Argentina 2 Iceland 1; Peru 2 Denmark 2; Croatia 1 Nigeria 0

Player to watch: Sisto. I realise I keep choosing guileful No.10s and wide attackers but couldn't resist a shout-out for Sisto. He was the star of the Midtjylland team that shocked Man U in the Europa League a couple of years ago and is thriving at Celta Vigo. The excitement levels rise when he picks up the ball

What happened next: Wins for Croatia and France, but Iceland held Argentina to a 1-1 draw and Denmark upset popular dark-horse pick Peru by a single goal. Sisto played in all of their games and was a speedy, exciting threat

Darts with Dele

So, yesterday, I played darts with Dele Alli. That's not an intro I ever expected to write but all bets are off with this new, touchy-feely, open, friendly England. As you might already know, the FA have rigged up a three-dart challenge between journalists and players, and I put myself forward to take on whoever they wanted to throw at me. I was actually confident about winning. Of course, I got thrashed. Some would say that's merely the pattern Scots follow at tournaments. Others that they'd expect nothing else when, at pretty much any sport, you pit a middle-aged bloke with limited grace against a brilliant young international athlete. Fair enough – but I fancied it.

On my day, I can throw a few okay arrows and in a quick practice throw I scored 134. But then Dele swept in, we did scissors-paper-stone as a 'toss' and my scissors shredded his paper. I chose to let him throw first and he casually hurled 53. I was envisaging having to beat something more like 26. And in the end 24 was my utterly pathetic score.

I learned two things. First, that Dele is a genuinely lovely lad. You quickly get a sense of people through the way they are in mundane interactions; the little moments, like introductions or small-talk situations. Dele was warm and down-to-earth. For two days at England practice in Zelengorosk he had been the last one signing autographs after a training session was over, so no surprise.

Second, just how hard it is to perform at sport under the spotlight. As anyone who has seen me on the oche at Sefton Park, my old cricket club in Liverpool, will testify, I am capable of bottling a darts match in a near-empty room, but this was a different experience. My game with Dele was being filmed live for TV and social media, and photographed for websites and newspapers. As I stepped to the oche I found myself staring at a forest of lenses, with about 30 staff and reporters also gathered round to watch. Suddenly my throwing arm felt incredibly tight and I dragged my first dart into the 3.

Mentality is one of the biggest things that separates elite footballers from the rest of us and Dele, despite showing little sign of actually having played darts (he threw naturally and smoothly but at seemingly random areas of the board), just had the mindset to grin, apply himself and thrive. And the stress of that darts match would have been about 0.0000000001% of what Dele faces whenever he steps on a pitch. (On Dele – an observer who has been very close to the England squad for over a decade told me today of his hunch that this will be Dele's tournament; he certainly looks in his best form all season and I love how much the role of attacking No.8 suits him. Spurs played him higher up the pitch – too high – last season.)

Touchy-feely, open, friendly England? All of us out here are writing about the new vibe. It feels enlightened. Happy. Chilled. Grown up. Players are opening up about their stories and emotions. Darts with the once-hated media is part of a Gareth Southgate-led process of removing barriers. "I remember, leading up to the Euros, it wasn't as relaxed and there was a lot more tension. And we all know what happened," says Marcus Rashford.

Will it help England on the pitch? You'd like to think so. But if it doesn't, and there is another failure, it should definitely help them deal with the aftermath. We, as a press, won't be writing sweet prose about them if they lose to Tunisia, but we understand this group of players as people better than any previous group, and I predict confidently the reaction will be more sympathetic and nuanced than for past disappointments. And the new environment has seen them bond closely as a unit: I would also trust them to bounce back from any setbacks better than any England squad.

Three rounds in, it's Players 3 Journalists 0. You can watch a video of Dele and myself... *https://goo.gl/6prUAs*

Predictions today: Brazil 4 Switzerland 1 Germany 2 Mexico 0; Costa Rica 0 Serbia 3

Player to watch: Sergej Milinkovic-Savic. From what I've seen and heard, this boy is a budding Dejan Stankovic. A slightly old-school player perhaps: creative, unhurried, technical in that classic Balkan style

What happened next: Brazil were held to a draw by Switzerland and Mexico delivered the shock of the first round, beating the world champions 1-0. Serbia only squeaked past Costa Rica; Lazio's Milinkovic-Savic played all three games as they bowed out after the group stage

Patriotism and Perspective

"Histiory is what it is," said Harry Kane yesterday, when played what they call a hospital pass with a question in his press conference about the deep meaning of being here in Volgograd. It wasn't the best answer, but then again I'm not sure how we journalists would do when put on the spot, the planet watching, about what the wars and atrocities of our forebears signify to us personally. And how it has a bearing on our day job. You never stop a bloke in an office and ask if he's pondering the Second World War while going through his morning emails. But these are the sorts of questions sportsmen face, fairly routinely.

"History is what it is" may not be the most sensitive comment in a location where at least two million perished during WW2's most bloody and pivotal battle. But Harry had a go, and it's better than John Terry's alleged response in a mixed zone to a question about the Malaysia Airlines Flight 370 disaster: "Well, obviously it's disappointing."

I'm just back from a morning visiting some of Volgograd's key monuments. There is 'The Motherland Calls', which is quite the most extraordinary memorial I have ever seen – an 85-metre, 8000-tonnes statue, the largest in the world of a woman. She stands on a hilltop, on a grass mound under which are buried hundreds of those who perished here. She looks down on the city rebuilt and renamed since it was Stalingrad, site of the key clash between the Soviets and Axis Alliance. 1.2m Soviet troops and 800,000 German, Italian and Romanian Alliance forces died in a 200-day battle, which ended in February 1943 with decisive Soviet victory. Hitler never recovered from his losses.

We also went to the city's war museum, with its stunning panorama depicting the battle. There were depictions of the gory reality of the fighting: the trenches, the snow, the air attacks, the hand-to-hand combat, the individual sacrifice. The soldier who threw his body in front of a machine gun so comrades could progress behind him; the officer who ran, body alight after a Molotov Cocktail exploded in his hand, to throw himself on a German tank and explode the second Molotov Cocktail he carried; the teenage pilot on his first flight who nosedived his plane into a German position in an act of kamikaze-style heroism. The Soviet women who became light tank commanders. And the snipers who helped the Soviets win the street fighting – "the score was 37,000 (Germans dead) for them," said our guide breezily.

Such sightseeing brings history alive and renews its meaning, but Harry Kane doesn't have time, here, to do that. "History is what it is" – he wanted to answer quickly and get back to concentrating on the football. And isn't that what we actually *want* him to be doing? Normally, I go to these places and don't do the war memorials. Some journalists and fans can't get enough of them. In my case, it's because I'm a little uneasy about the whole relationship between sport and war and constant efforts to tie them together. Yet I loved history at school and believe firmly that our past in this world gets too much forgotten. In other words, I haven't quite worked things out – a bit like Harry. So who would I be to make fun of him?

Gareth Southgate is the first England manager I've seen to express English patriotism (a thorny subject) confidently yet with perspective. Gareth, whose grandad, a marine commando, was his hero, has brought in amputee soldiers to speak to England players and taken them training with the Royal Marines, and he wants them to play with pride for their country. Yet he manages to do all this without jingoism and with due respect to the patriotism and different perspectives of other nations. I think I like him because his vibe is "being English is great" rather than "being English is best".

Anyway, here's a football/military cliche: The Phony War is Over. Yep, at last all the talking about England is done and it is time for football. I fancy they'll be okay against Tunisia tonight, though the Tunisians will pose plenty difficulties. As will the heat here in Volgograd. And the damn flies.

Predictions today: Sweden 1 South Korea 0; Belgium 5 Panama 1; England 2 Tunisia 0

Player to watch: Dele Alli. Have a feeling that, fresh from the confidence boost I gave him on the oche, this is going to be a breakthrough tournament for him

What happened next: Sweden, Belgium and England all won – although the Three Lions left it late against Tunisia. Dele Alli improved as the tournament progressed and his reputation continues to grow – both as a daring midfielder and a fearless arrowsman

The World Cup So Far

After spraffing (an Irvine Welsh word) about darts and war in my last two entries, I thought I'd best get back to the football. So here, with the first round of games ending today, are some observations about the tournament up to now.

Stars Under Pressure

It was telling Harry Kane referenced Cristiano Ronaldo in his press conference in Volgograd. He talked about Ronaldo setting a target with his hat-trick v Spain, and his ambition to match it. This is very much how modern footballers see things: themselves as solo entities, big brands, in competition with other solo stars, that struggle being almost as important as the competition between respective teams.

The nature of how people follow the game is changing, especially among a younger generation. Thanks to FIFA, thanks to marketing, thanks to society's focus on the individual – on personal image and a person's self-fulfilment – kids 'support' single players as much as they do clubs and national sides. If you doubt this, and are brave enough, drop by Twitter and try entering the Ronaldo v Messi debate. The partisanship there is as fierce and nasty as club rivalry.

I think this impacts on the footballers themselves. Zinedine Zidane, Roberto Baggio, George Weah, the Brazilian Ronaldo … these guys, the superstars of the recent past, didn't obsess about the Ballon D'Or or other individual honours the way Ronaldo, Messi and Neymar do. At the World Cup, you can see in play the pressure upon individual stars to be No.1. Ronaldo's ego fuelled him to an almost miraculous 90 minutes v Spain, but when Messi and Neymar played both seemed as if they were trying just a bit too hard. There wasn't the clarity in their games you see when they're at their best. They were shooting too much from distance, banging free-kicks into walls, holding possession just a little too long. Was the expectation upon them to 'do a Ronaldo' a factor in their play?

It was interesting how well Kane and Romelu Lukaku began the tournament. They are also in competition, two young strikers who vie with each other in the Premier League and are now in Russia hoping these finals will catapult them to the next level of global stardom. Rom 2 Harry 2. Fascinated to see who goes further here and emerges from a four-way battle (with Timo Werner and Gabriel Jesus also involved) to be the coming man.

Var-dly Used

It seems less is more when it comes to FIFA's approach with VAR here. The video assistants are not intervening nearly as much as expected and I think that's largely a good thing. Albeit that Kane should have had at least one penalty last night. When VARs have been used they have generally helped refs reach the right decisions, like Sweden's pen against South Korea, which I thought was a dive before the replays uncovered the foul.

What I don't like is when VAR gets involved in marginal calls. What's the point, when it's a 50-50 decision, in changing from one debatable position to the equally debatable alternative? Sadly this has happened a couple of times, for example with France's penalty in their 2-1 win against Australia. Read the laws of football and you will see just how inexact, unspecific and therefore open to interpretation they are. Refereeing will always be subjective. VAR can only help with the glaring errors. It cannot achieve a perfectly officiated game.

Nothing To Fear

Having watched all the tournament favourites in action, England can say they have nothing to fear. Then again, I don't think any of the favourites will be quaking after seeing England. Only Spain have played really special football and even then I'm only talking about the attacking half of their game. With Gerard Pique, David De Gea and to a lesser extent Sergio Busquets off-key v Portugal, the defensive side of their play was average. Only Sergio Ramos held them together at the back. This World Cup is shaping up like the 2006 one: no outstanding side, no 'big beast' – an open tournament. Maybe clearer favourites will emerge as the group stage evolves. While watching out for a likely winner, remember one thing: World Cups are nearly always won by the big side that concedes the fewest goals.

The Absolute State of Russian TV

A personal highlight of Euro 2016 was watching French television cover their own tournament. So many cultural differences. They had this weird/arty/cheesy/brilliant thing where the French man of the match, or Didier Deschamps, was interviewed straight after the match at the stadium and 'projected' into the studio as a hologram. David Ginola suavely bantering with a virtual Dmitri Payet? What's not to like?

Russian coverage is endearingly batty. At half-time, instead of po-faced studio analysis, they go straight into some kind of Russian Soccer AM with models wearing hats or colours representing the teams playing, and a whole load of frothy chat. Top bantz comrades!

Predictions today: Poland 2 Senegal 2; Colombia 1 Japan 0; Russia 0 Egypt 1

Player to watch: Mo Salah. He has to play today, Egypt have a World Cup campaign to save. All eyes will be on him, including mine, and you hope he gets protection and that VAR gets involved if defenders try to manhandle him and snidely test that injured shoulder. If he's anything like fit, he can terrify the plodding Russian defence, old Ignashevich especially, with his speed and movement. Going back to the theme of star players, here is one who could really lift an already fine tournament if he shines

What happened next: An early red card cost Colombia as they went down to Japan, while Senegal impressed in a 2-1 win over Poland. Russia continued to surprise – they were 3-1 winners against Egypt, but Salah did grab his goal, from the spot, one of two in his two matches at the tournament

World Cup Level

When Manchester United went to Moscow to play CSKA in the 2015-16 Champions League, a local journalist asked Louis Van Gaal about Marcos Rojo. How could it be that someone who was abject when he played in the Russian league could now be playing for Man U?

"What?" said Van Gaal. Old Louis appeared completely unaware that Rojo had spent two seasons stinking out the place at Spartak Moscow, prior to moving to Sporting Lisbon, from who United signed him. Van Gaal, never a man to stand corrected, batted away the journalist's account of Rojo's Russian nightmare, which consisted of a miserable 17 appearances in two seasons. Who cares, Louis said. "I knew what he could do because of the World Cup."

Yep, it appears LVG bought Rojo on a similar whim that made Sir Alex Ferguson buy Karel Poborsky after Euro 96. He'd done well at a tournament. But what does that mean? I grew up hearing the phrase 'World Cup level' as reference to the highest echelon of the game. Well, this is my sixth World Cup as a journalist and I can tell you that it is ... and it isn't ... the highest level.

I was thinking about 'World Cup level' at the St Petersburg Stadium last night, watching Russia v Egypt. Russia are like a Neil Warnock team, smacking it high and direct, winning the 50-50s and second balls, running the channels, and hitting the opposition with long throws and even longer diagonals. Their striker, Artem Dzyuba looks and plays a bit like Richard Dunne. It's like watching a team who has decided to throw its centre-half upfield in desperate search of goal ... for the whole 90 minutes.

Egypt were not much more sophisticated, another direct team with a big striker. They would make a cursory attempt to pass the ball around at the back, but then one of their full-backs would launch it up the line. They were trying to go Route One to Mo Salah at several points. All in all, it was something like watching Cardiff v Middlesbrough.

World Cup level? Technique-wise, tactics-wise, many games at this tournament don't compare to the Premier League, La Liga or Bundesliga. The Champions League has long replaced the World Cup as football's ultimate level in terms of quality. We've kind of stopped asking that age-old question 'Would Brazil beat Real Madrid?' Pause for a moment and envision England playing Manchester City. Ouch.

International teams will never match club sides in certain ways. An obvious one is personnel, for clubs can buy and blend talent from around the world. In a sense, Manchester City have 7.4 billion people to choose from, whereas England have just 53 million. Clubs can attract the best coaches and, increasingly, the very top managers avoid international management or wait until the end of their careers. Clubs can get their players fitter and better-drilled because of the far greater training time. Look out for how few teams at the World Cup are deploying proper pressing games.

Look at some of those who have 'starred' at World Cups. Rojo did do well in 2014 for Argentina, as did Martin Demichelis and Sergio Romero. They were minutes from taking Germany to a penalty shoot-out in the final. But Real Madrid were never going to be knocking on their doors. Third place in 2014 were Holland, managed by LVG himself. That success was seen as evidence of Van Gaal being revitalised as a coach, but his subsequent stint at

United proved he was actually out of gas. And just ponder this: Ron Vlaar and Michel Vorm have World Cup bronze medals. Yep. And Jordi Clasie, Bruno Martins Indi, Daryl Janmaat, Jonathan De Guzman too.

And yet the World Cup *is* the highest level in another sense. Nowhere else are players under such pressure. Nowhere else are they so 'alone' in the sense of being cut off from their families, agents, club support systems, routines, familiar training patterns and, obviously, the club coaches and team-mates who are part of their success. For stars, they are playing for teams much worse than they're used to (Ronaldo with Portugal, Messi with Argentina) so it's down to them. A player really does stand or fall by their own efforts and character at a World Cup.

Which is why the most cherished achievements are such as Maradona in 1986, Zidane in 1998, Pele in 1970: those times when players eclipse a whole tournament and take glory through their supreme talents and personalities. Brazil 70 may have been the greatest team of all time, yet Pele, by then a veteran, having begun his World Cup story as a remarkable 17-year-old scoring twice in the 1958 final, still bestrode everything.

Predictions today: Portugal 1 Morocco 1; Uruguay 3 Saudi Arabia 0; Spain 1 Iran 0

Player to watch: David De Gea. Unquestionably the world's best goalkeeper, but something does not seem right with him. His howler against Portugal came after a mistake v Switzerland in one of the warm-up games. He has fallen out with the Spanish prime minister and faced the usual questions about Real Madrid. But cheer up Dave, you get to train with Iniesta and not Marcos Rojo when you're with your country

What happened next: A single goal was all Uruguay could muster against Saudi Arabia. Portugal beat Morocco 1-0, and Spain grabbed the same result against Iran thanks to Diego Costa. As for De Gea – few elite players saw their reputation take as big a blow as the Spain keeper

New School

Yesterday evening in Repino there was a drinks thing for journos and FA people. It was at a beach bar where a few nights ago there was a Russian stag party at which a stripper leapt out of a giant cake. I wasn't there, but having seen how popular collagen and silicone are in these parts (villas on this coast are bolt-holes for the *nouveau riche* and their WAGs – it is even rumoured Putin has a place), I wasn't surprised to hear about it.

Anyway, we turned up at the beach bar to hear from the FA that drinks would be delayed because "a major England story was about to break". We rushed back to our media hotel to await the announcement, speculating on what kind of story it could be.

Was it merely an update on the quad injury Dele Alli picked up against Tunisia?

Had someone failed a drugs test?

Fabien Delph going home for his wife's labour?

What was Vardy up to?

Had some sozzled FA blazer from the counties 'liked' Lord Sugar's atrocious Senegal tweet? (Beside a photo of the Senegal team, accompanied by another of sunglasses and handbags laid out for sale, he tweeted: "I recognise some of these guys from the beach in Marbella. Multi tasking resourceful chaps." You're fired by the way, Sugar. No more *The Apprentice* for me.)

It turned out to be no more than Gareth Southgate dislocating his shoulder while out for a 10km run. He stumbled while going too fast trying to beat his personal record. Now, the reaction was interesting. Not long ago a story like that would have been front-page stuff. The news guys and snappers would have been sent straight to the England hotel. The pun headlines would have been in overdrive (today's *Mirror* did go for Sling When You're Winning, which is good). And hacks would have sat round brewing up fake indignation about an England manager letting down his country by doing something that might impair him in training and on the bench.

There was none of that. The first question my pal, Rob Draper, from the *Mail on Sunday*, asked was "wonder what Gareth's 10km PB is? Wouldn't mind trying to beat it." And what followed were discussions about running, cycling, the gym and the difficulty of trying to stay fit at a tournament. *The Telegraph's* excellent Sam Wallace was the first journalist I heard described as 'new school' (he still has the nickname 'school'). This was because, on trips, Sam was always healthy, always looking to minimise the drinking side, get early nights and stay fit. And Sam still looks about 30, so fair play.

There are some very fit and healthy journos in the pack now. I wouldn't like to take on Matt Lawton or Neil Ashton on a bike, and would have my work cut out against Lawton, Ashton, Matt Hughes, Matt Dickinson, and especially Rob in a road race. As a young journalist, the challenges on these trips used to be keeping up with the other guys at the bar. Now it's trying to match their Strava stats. We have changed as a pack and England managers have changed too.

- Gareth: His parents met at a school athletics meet and he goes running with his dogs near Harrogate. A guy from a very athletic family, who at 47 looks like he could still play. Hobbies: the outdoors, family, being fit

- Roy Hodgson: Missed scouting Iceland in order to go

on a boat trip down the Seine with Ray Lewington. Different generation

- Big Sam: "Red wine please. A pint."
- Fabio Capello: Busy updating his sponsored Capello Index and angling for Serie A jobs during the build-up and tournament in 2010. Well, £6m per year from the FA isn't much to live on…
- Schteve McClaren: Just seemed to spend the whole time fretting. And getting wet
- Sven Goran Eriksson: Not the sober Swede we expected. The little detail about his built-up shoes left outside the bedroom door – from Faria Alam's kiss-and-tell – will forever stay with me

So, we're different and so are England managers these days.

Predictions today: Denmark 2 Australia 1; France 1 Peru 1; Argentina 1 Croatia 1

Player to watch: Lionel Messi. What a big game it is for him this evening. I'm not of the opinion that he has anything to prove at the World Cup. His greatness is beyond question. But it looks like Ronaldo is going to win another Ballon, and that he will always live with those World Cup question marks unless he and Argentina can do something here

What happened next: Denmark and Australia duked out a 1-1 draw; France sneaked past Peru 1-0 and Croatia announced their candidacy for the title with a stunning 3-0 win over Messi's Argentina. The little genius had his moments in Russia, but left without ever looking like a possible winner

— Day Nine, June 22
Messi v Ronaldo, Ronaldo v Messi

I am about to do something that I would never be daft enough to do on Twitter: enter the Messi v Ronaldo debate. Maybe it's because last night was the longest night of the year in St Petersburg, with only about two hours of semi-twilight from 2am-4am before it seemed day-time again. I didn't sleep (despite my eye-guard) and fatigue may be clouding my judgment here.

But let's give it a go…

Ronaldo v Messi is tribal. Social media fosters tribalism and black-or-white opinions in all sorts of spheres and football is no exception. Marketing also keeps asking us to choose between rival stars' brands and Ronaldo v Messi is football's version of Pepsi v Coke. I doubt previous generations were at each other's throats over whether Stanley Matthews was superior to Tom Finney, or Johan Cruyff surpassed Franz Beckenbauer. Twenty years ago, some people would have said Zidane was the world's best player, others that it was Brazilian Ronaldo, some may have even chosen Luis Figo and there was no Twitter for anyone to issue death threats. I've never bothered with Messi v Ronaldo on that space, but let's have a go here.

This is all sparked by watching Messi have probably one of the worst games of his career and certainly one of the worst nights of his career in Argentina's 3-0 defeat by Croatia. The Croatians were brilliant by the way, what a midfield they possess, and what a player Dejan Lovren can be when he's inspired. I was watching in the common room at the media hotel in Repino and as Modric shaped to shoot I said loudly: "He can't score!" Good job I don't analyse football for a living. Anyway, last night summed up Messi's international career and therefore his flaws.

His problems...

- Argentina are an absurdly lopsided team, with (even taking Messi out of it), world-class attacking talent and lower-Premier-League-class defensive players. Plus a moderate midfield.
- Argentina have chopped and changed tactics and coaches continually for the last decade.
- Argentina, and their current generation, are psychologically bruised by a sequence of near misses in Copa Americas and the last World Cup.
- Beyond the Messi/Aguero generation there are much more ordinary younger players coming through. Not many of the players are good enough to start or be effective when they do. This robs the older lot of badly needed pace and legs around them.
- Willy Caballero is one of the loveliest footballers I've ever met, with a heart-rending backstory ... but no, I wouldn't have him in goal either.
- Jorge Sampaoli's high-octane pressing, counter-attacking, hit-em-with-width tactics are exactly wrong for the profile of the current squad.
- Judging by the look he is trying to rock in Russia, Sampaoli clearly reveres Pitbull. Now, Pitbull may want to just "stop time" and "feel the moment" because "that *chico* nice" but Messi could do with a bit more planning and structure from his coach.

However, I could compile a list of Portugal's problems and (Pitbull aside) they wouldn't be dramatically different.

Unbalanced squad, moderate defenders, a little lacking in legs. The differences would be: better goalkeeper, better coach (or coach better suited to the team). But you have to recognise that Ronaldo faces obstacles when he turns out for his country, too. So why is Ronaldo doing so much better than Messi at this World Cup, and has been doing better in international football for the last three or four years?

I've watched both at tournaments and what I'd conclude is this. Ronaldo's great asset is his ego, his sense of destiny, his self-importance, his unshakable confidence in himself as a matchwinner and difference-maker. He is like Michael Jordan, who told team-mates to always give him the ball in the final seconds. He wanted to be the guy with the ball when there was just one shot to win the game. This is Ronaldo's mentality and because of it he is perhaps the best big-game player the world has seen, or at very least on a par with Maradona and Pele (who were extraordinary in World Cup tournaments) in this regard. Just go back through the Champions League finals and the crunch games for Portugal, plus his Clasico record. Where others shrink, Ronaldo grows. The pressure on Ronaldo when he plays for Portugal is different to the onus on Messi with Argentina. For Ronaldo it is positive pressure. His country are looking to him, but even if he fails he is still their hero, their No.1 of all time. He can only enhance his legend, not damage it.

For Messi, even if he wins the World Cup single-handedly, he will never be No.1 for many compatriots. That's Maradona. He *has* to win the World Cup just to make par. Because he left his country as a child to sign for Barcelona, neither does he have the embedded support that comes from having served time in his nation's domestic league. He has retired and unretired. Psychologically it is difficult for him.

But what about technically? Is there a reason Ronaldo does better than Messi? Well I wonder two things: Ronaldo is a supreme counter-attacking player – if a computer designed a counter-attacking forward it would probably come out with Ronaldo's attributes. And counter-attack play tends to work better than possession football in knockout competitions, from the World Cup to the Champions League to domestic cups. Or at least it seems to, when I look at recent winners and those through history. So this is Ronaldo's environment, Ronaldo's scene.

Ronaldo, from childhood, has been developed as an individual player. A star. A soloist. First as 'The Stepover King' and arch-dribbler of his early professional years. Then as the *uber* goalscorer. Messi, on the other hand, was schooled at *La Masia,* where the entire curriculum is team work, team play, team pattern. Part of his genius is being able to work as a matchwinner supreme while also working as a cog in the Barcelona system. He is undoubtedly a more complete player than CR7: a better passer, a greater orchestrator of play, as well as being the better dribbler and having the superior touch. But all this means that CR7 is programmed to be able to prevail as an individual. Messi less so. Behind him he needs a team.

I only fully understood how good Messi is at the 2014 World Cup. I'd seen him, live, in Champions League matches for Barcelona, play with mesmerising brilliance in the final third of the pitch. But in 2014, in Brasilia, I watched him drop into his own half and strike the best pass I have ever witnessed in the flesh, to Angel Di Maria. I'll remember it forever: it was a moment beyond genius, that showed his range. Pushed, I'd say Messi is the greater footballer than Ronaldo. But in the latter phase of his career, Ronaldo is challenging everything we thought we knew about him (and by proxy his rival), and I'd have to conclude Ronaldo is the greater sportsman. The winner's gene which powers him is that of a Michael Jordan, a Federer, a Tiger Woods. It is his common ground with the greats of other sports. Does this leave me sitting on the fence? I don't know. I'm more confident in other debates: Brian Lara was better than Tendulkar, Ali than Tyson and of course Willie Miller beats Alan Hansen any day.

So, Ronaldo or Messi? I'm going to end up giving the same answer I always do. Pele.

Predictions today: Brazil 3 Costa Rica 0; Nigeria 0 Iceland 1; Serbia 1 Switzerland 1

Player to watch: Kari Arnason. The best player in Iceland's defence as they muzzled Messi in their opening game and an absolutely outstanding performer for his country. Yet spent most of last season on the bench for Aberdeen and in his biggest game of the season was all over the place against Motherwell. Mind you, have you seen Motherwell? They look, and play, like a prison team

What happened next: Brazil put two past Costa Rica, Switzerland beat Serbia in a politically-charged encounter and Nigeria impressed in a 2-0 win over Iceland. Kari Arnason's performance against Messi won the 35-year-old a move to Genclerbirligi, aborting a summer move back to Iceland to switch to the Turkish side

— Day 10, June 23
The Mixed Zone

Welcome to Matchday Minus 1. And to FIFA-speak. Matchday Minus 1 is their inimitably bureaucratic way of saying 'the day before the game'. I'm in Nizhny Novgorod with England ahead of tomorrow's game with Panama. It was a 3.30am start, to get a bus from Repino, a flight from St Petersburg and then another flight from Moscow, before a bus to the stadium, to get there in time for Gareth Southgate's Matchday Minus 1 press conference. 3.30am! It's Matchday Minus 1, minus sleep.

Another bit of FIFA-speak is 'mixed zone'. Or is it a UEFA phrase? I can't remember. I first encountered it at some tournament, long ago. The mixed zone is where the business end of today's work will be for reporters from English Sunday newspapers. Southgate's press conference is open to the world's media and will be broadcast, streamed and tweeted everywhere, which is no use to us. The content will be old by the time our papers come out. So, thanks to the considerateness of the FA (who have to negotiate permission with FIFA, because FIFA don't like things happening outside their official media schedule), we're getting access to Gareth separately.

I thought I'd write a wee bit about mixed zones because you may have read or heard journalists use the phrase and wondered what they look like and how they work.

First things first. "The mixed zone" suggests some kind of ... mixing. Perhaps a social space. Some sort of mingling opportunity, maybe even with players, managers and journos having nibbles and clinking drinks. Forget that. A mixed zone is actually all about separation. About strictly *no* mixing. There's a barrier, behind which we stand, and a walkway, down which the talent passes. We shout, beg, hector, pester, try cheesy charm in an effort to make them stop and jizz a few minutes of quotes into our dictaphones. The majority decline and sometimes, looking at our desperation, the way we crowd over the barriers, elbowing aside rival groups of reporters, you sympathise. The whole thing is demeaning to us, and demeaning to them.

I was in the mixed zone after Russia v Egypt. Salah didn't stop (no surprise, he's very private and never does). But we were optimistic about speaking to one of the Russian players, given the high they were on after their victory. I messaged John Bradley, who commentates on Russian football, to ask which Russians speak English and John replied with a list. Yuri Zhirkov, lovely fella, old pro, two years with Chelsea. John and I agreed that he was the banker. Yuri duly walked past. "I'm sorry guys, but I do not speak English," he replied. In perfect English.

Artem Dzyuba was another on John's list. A similar interaction. He was in a good mood though, and as he walked away from us (a gaggle of five or six British hacks) he said something that sounded awfully like "pricks". Dzyuba is 6'5 and looks like he has eaten Richard Dunne – and he was also clearly still pumped with the ... um ... definitely natural adrenaline ... that's been powering those Russia players. So we didn't call him back to clarify.

Zhirkov's language gambit? Used all the time. One of the oldest excuses from foreign players who don't want to stop. But British players are just as adept at fobbing us off. Here are some other excuses...

- The player walks past, seemingly talking on their mobile phone. What a shame lads, would love to stop, but just gotta take this call. An England player, who I won't embarrass, was caught out doing this. One of the lads had his number and called him as he walked by, phone to his ear and 'talking'. The phone rang.

- The players walk through in a large group, really fast and purposeful, as if the team bus is waiting or they've a squad thing to go to. Then they get to the end and mysteriously all urgency disappears as they hang with their wash bags and entourages, chatting.

- Didi Hamann had a beauty, which he used for two consecutive Champions League mixed zones at Anfield. He came through munching on a bun. Sorry lads, mouth is full, it's this nice bun, you see? Refuelling and all of that. The first time it seemed fair enough. The second time, knowing Didi and his off-beat ways, you knew he was at it.

- Michael Ballack pulled a world-class variation of the language ruse on me. This was 2001-02, when Leverkusen faced Liverpool and then Manchester United in quick succession. After the Liverpool game in Germany, me and another reporter, Jim Holden, hung around the BayArena players' car park and grabbed Ballack on his way to his sleek black Audi. He was good as gold, spoke charmingly for five minutes. Two weeks later I saw him at Old Trafford. "Hi Michael, can I have a quick word?" He smiled. "Sorry, I don't speak English." But you spoke English two weeks ago Michael. "Yes," Ballack grinned, "but that was two weeks ago."

Every team, however, has stalwart mixed-zone stoppers. Players the press love, guys who will always give you five minutes, even if they've already done three or four other interviews. Andy Robertson would be Liverpool's current mixed-zone king. At Manchester United it was Michael Carrick, but now he's retired it's probably Chris Smalling or Ander Herrera. No one at Arsenal really stops at all these days. Tottenham are organised and designate players to stop by rota. At Chelsea you can bank on Gary Cahill and usually get Willian. Leicester? Marc Albrighton, all day long.

Manchester City have my personal mixed-zone hero. It's Fernandinho. I was at Brazil's 7-1 defeat by Germany in 2014 in Belo Horizonte and the Brazilians, having experienced the greatest humiliation in their country's football history, were understandably in bits. There were tears, ashen faces, zombie expressions: they were the walking dead. But Fernandinho, magnificent, brave, decent, Fernandinho, stopped and gave interviews even though he faced some of the biggest criticism of all for his performance.

A career low point was being snubbed in a mixed zone in Dallas by Franco Di Santo on a Chelsea US tour. I only asked him because he was a kid and I felt sorry for him because he wasn't playing and nobody else was bothering to try to stop him. But, haughtily, he waved me away and then began doing keepy-ups with a spare ball. I was so pleased when he was freed by Wigan.

Anyway, off to the big Nizhny mixed zone. Wish me luck.

PS: The talking-on-the-phone trick works a treat when you need to walk past market research people, or those in charity bibs in the town centre. But here's a tip: call your own voicemail, so the phone doesn't ring.

Predictions today: Belgium 0 Tunisia 0; South Korea 0 Mexico 1; Germany 2 Sweden 1

Player to watch: Hirving Lozano. Brilliant in Mexico's win over Germany and now being linked to Barcelona. Had a brilliant season with PSV and is 22 yet has already played a lot of football at a good level. At a tournament you're always looking to see if such a player is a one-game star or can maintain their standard of performance

What happened next: Belgium thrashed Tunisia 5-2; Germany did indeed win 2-1 – albeit after losing Jerome Boateng to a red card – and Mexico won again. Manchester United joined Barcelona in the hunt for Lozano after an impressive World Cup for the attacker

A good moment. "We are in a good moment." It is something you often hear foreign players and managers say. In English the phrase does not exactly make sense, but I like it. It gives a sense of things coming together at a point in time, of being in that sweet spot that is so important in sport. Often, the foreign guys use it to refer to confidence or form: a 'good moment' of performance. But I find it useful when thinking about development. You look at a team or player and try to view them within the context of their evolution. What kind of moment are they in, good or bad? What point have they reached in their journey?

I've been thinking about this in regard to Germany. At the start of this blog I said I felt the Germans were over-rated, because their best players were just passing or had already passed their best and their opening two games only strengthened my view. They survived last night v Sweden (scoring the latest goal, excluding extra-time situations, in German World Cup history). It was thanks to a wonderful strike from Toni Kroos, a woeful wall lined up by the Swedes (just two men?!) and that fabled *Mannschaft* mentality.

But clearly, Germany are a team still in trouble. They were almost dumped out of the World Cup by Ola Toivonen, who didn't score for Toulouse in 23 games last season and failed to net a single goal in a season-long loan at the Stadium of Light. "A 150-year-old tortoise brought to Britain by Darwin and then mysteriously signed by Sunderland," is how one Black Cats fan described big Ola on Twitter.

What was fascinating about Germany was how, right at the death, right when they needed to, they suddenly looked like *Germany* again during those last few minutes of play, and think about this: They went to the World Cup leaving out Leroy Sane and several of the talented young players who did so well for them at the Confederations Cup; Joachim Low's plan was to go again with the old guard, the heroes who were first winners at the Under-21 Euros in 2009 and went all the way to being world champions in 2014.

Low started with all his go-to guys in the first game v Mexico. They were slow, tired, pathetically out-paced when Mexico counter-attacked. They looked like the press team when we were hammered by the slick Ukrainians before the Champions League final in Kiev. Or worse: England at the 2010 World Cup.

Low is not stupid (clearly) and took action, dropping half the old guard for the Sweden game. Out went Mats Hummels, Mesut Ozil, Sami Khedira. Germany moved the ball and worked out of possession quicker. But there was still a staleness in their play.

Jerome Boateng, another old guard player, was ordered off in the 82nd minute. Germany then ... improved. Julian Brandt came on and made an enormous difference. Antonio Rudiger had a very valuable game. Joshua Kimmich looked the best footballer on the pitch (barring the man I'm about to talk about). *Most* of the best guys were the young guys...

Toni Kroos: Now, when Germany had their great finale against the Swedes there were just three 2014 world champions left on the pitch. Neuer, Muller ... and Kroos. A huge shift from where Low was at the start of the tournament. And Kroos is not really an 'old guard' player, because he's younger than the 2009 crew, came through a little later, was seen as a slight outsider by Germans in his younger days (different personality/mentality) and left Germany early, committing the 'sin' of ditching Bayern Munich. He was always the junior member of the 2014 crew.

But Kroos is Germany's best player and I felt that a big factor last night was that at the end, at long last, Germany became Toni Kroos' team. *He* was the main man. He was leading the orchestra, he was the dominant guy on the pitch, and there was a nice balance of experience (Mario Gomez, Marco Reus) and youth (Brandt, Kimmich, Rudiger) around him. He needed that platform within the context of the match because it was his mistake that led to Sweden scoring, and he was on a mission to make up for it. But he also probably needed it in the context of his career. And, to go back to my original point – at last Germany were moving on. At last Germany were no longer stale. At last Germany were evolving. Germany had found that better *moment*.

Staleness, not age, is the enemy in sport. An old player can still be fresh (look at Cristiano Ronaldo). A young player can be complacent, their development atrophied. A team can be at its peak on paper (the average age of Low's old guard is around 28) but past it in reality.

Old champions need youth around them. Fergie was a master at bringing youth into his teams, continually refreshing them. He loved being around young players and young people because he understood the value, as he got older, of interacting with youthful personalities. You speak to Giggs and Scholes, and even Ferdinand, Vidic or Carrick – slightly different generations of older United players – and the affection all of them had for the young Ronaldo is clear. He was this daft, egotistical, brilliant boy in their midst and he helped keep them fresh. Wayne Rooney did, too.

Fergie always said football was like a bus and you had to decide whether you wanted to stay on it or get off. And getting off was fatal. A bus always moving forward, travelling onwards ... you had to keep moving too.

What moment are England in? A good one. They are evolving, hitting form. They're probably too young to win anything, but this World Cup might prove a valuable staging post.

I have fancied Spain from the start because they have that right blend of older stars and young players. The Kokes and Iscos are ensuring the team of Andres Iniesta and David Silva is still moving forward. Brazil are at a good stage too, no staleness there. Croatia, Belgium have good dynamics. The thing about Germany is that there is no nation better at fixing problems and re-engineering, and far from stupid, Low is a clever man. He may well recognise what we've seen in the first two games and start with a team close to the one that finished the Sweden game. Then that German bus will be moving forward again.

Predictions today: England 3 Panama 0; Japan 0 Senegal 2; Poland 2 Colombia 3

Kalidou Koulibaly (Senegal): Tough defender, lovely footballer, super athlete. The World Cup has not seen many great displays by defenders but if Senegal stay in, this guy can be one of the players of the tournament. Perfect attributes for a centre-back in the modern game. No wonder Mauricio Sarri wants to take him with him to Chelsea

What happened next: England battered Panama 6-1 as Harry Kane scored a hat-trick; Colombia arrived at the World Cup with a 3-0 win over Poland; Japan twice came from behind to draw with Senegal. Koulibaly elected to remain at Napoli, signing a new five-year deal after the close season

— Day 12, June 25
Russia Today

Greetings and *preevyet* from seat 24A on Aeroflot SU14 from Moscow to St Petersburg. It's our eighth flight in eight days and we have now transited through Moscow Sheremetyevo Airport Terminal D four times. Yep, it's getting to that point in a trip where you become institutionalised and start counting such things (and if you think *that* was a dull intro, be thankful I haven't regaled you with the conversations football reporters have about motorways and favourite service stations).

So, it was another early start – 3.5 hours of sleep again. Those .5s become vital when you're fighting tiredness like this. At Sheremetyevo I downed a flat white (second of the day) and a green smoothie, in hope they will magically restore my brain function. I'm actually surprised I'm managing to hold the laptop up the right way. Since leaving our hotel in Nizhny Novgorod at 6am I've already left my phone in the back of a taxi (thankfully, for 1000 roubles the fella came back to the airport with it).

The Uzbek restaurant with its craft beer, and then that one last 'Astrolager' in the bar round the corner might have something to do with it. Nizhny, it transpires, is a great night out; a brilliant city. Lively. Fun people. Some of the lads were out in a bar on Saturday where a Russian ska band, complete with pork pie hats, had the whole place skanking. I was in a cab coming back from working late at the stadium at that point: the young lad driving my beat-up Lada Yandex (a Russian version of *Uber*) had some vintage Busta Rhymes smacking it up on his stereo.

Upon reaching my hotel we did The Receipt Thing,

a routine played out daily in every corner of the world, where expenses-hungry travelling journo haggles for receipt with driver of unofficial cab, who clearly does not put his journeys through any kind of books. My driver last night was a nice lad, so I gave up quickly (the fare was four quid, I'll take the hit). He didn't have change of my 500 roubles and rummaged around in his glove compartment before producing a glossy, plastic 100 roubles bill.

Then he started typing in his phone, painstakingly and solemnly. He was using a translation app and eventually showed me the screen. His translated message said: "I am sorry. There are no tickets available for this kind of journey. Please accept. This is not signified currency, it is souvenir note. It can be your memory." How could I refuse? We thumbs-upped and off he and Busta went into the night. Of course I've lost the note already. Left it in the hotel room this morning when trying to get up and dressed within seven minutes after 3.5 hours sleep.

Anyway, Nizhny turned out to be a hidden gem. Don't think I'll ever be back, but I'm glad I went. And Russia itself is turning out to be brilliant. The people, so far, have been lovely. The weather's great, food good. Uzbek cuisine turns out to be very like Turkish, though the best dish of last night's meal reminded me of home. It was fried mutton pie.

Fried.

Mutton.

Pie.

Pretty much the Holy Trinity for a Scot.

The relatively small number of England fans here seem to be having a great time and not just because of their team's football.

Wanted to write a bit about Russia today because the country is proving to be so different to the one portrayed in our scare-mongering security briefings. They told us it was ridden with violence and corruption; would be hostile to British journalists; dangerous and difficult at every turn. Oh and that every Russian could be some kind of spy. Well, the young guy who came over to chat at the Astrolager-selling bar didn't seem KGB. Unless gabbing about CSKA Moscow and yelling "my Akinfeeeev is No.1!" was an elaborate cover. Russia is cool, not like we were told and the same happened with Brazil, South Africa. Don't believe British suspicion and negativity. I retain plenty reservations about Russia hosting, from the corrupt bidding process, to drug-cheating, to Putin and soft power. But if the point of taking this tournament to different corners of the world is to break down national barriers, then on a person-to-person basis Russia 2018 is working.

Right, there's not been much football in today's post, so here are my favourite goals from the second round of group games.

- Yerry Mina (Columbia) v Poland: Superb team goal and towering header to finish
- Jesse Lingard (England) v Panama: Gorgeous interplay and a sweet finish from an unsung hero of the team
- Granit Xhaka (Switzerland) v Serbia: Beautiful strike, powered in unerring and a moment that meant so much politically and personally to him
- Ahmed Musa (Nigeria) v Iceland: The one where he catches it on his toe and half-volleys it in. He looks a talent. Leicester should sign him
- Toni Kroos (Germany) v Sweden: Great players do it in the moments that count
- Luka Modric (Croatia) v Argentina: Fabulous strike by one of my favourite players

- Eden Hazard (Belgium) v Tunisia: Not the penalty, the other goal. The touch, my word, the touch to nick it past the keeper

Predictions today: Russia 1 Uruguay 1; Egypt 2 Saudi Arabia 1; Spain 2 Morocco 0; Portugal 1 Iran 0

Player to watch: Koke. Knits that Spanish midfield together with his industry and is the kind of player other players love having alongside them. I fancy Spain to go far and he could become one of their most important players

What happened next: Saudi Arabia went home with a World Cup win after beating Egypt 2-1, while Russia ran out of gas as they went down 3-0 to Uruguay. Then in a night of VAR-based drama, Portugal and Iran drew 1-1, but Spain nicked top spot after a 2-2 draw with Morocco. Koke was part of a midfield coming under increasing criticism for a lack of incisiveness

— *Day 13, June 26*
Models and Messi

I think I'm going to stand up Miss Russia. The jauntiest of emails landed in my inbox this morning. It began, "Happy Monday!" (Shaun Ryder writing to me again?) and the exclamation marks kept coming. "I understand you are currently in Russia covering The World Cup!" and "I would be happy to answer any queries!" As Colin Hendry once told me in an interview, lowering his great craggy face as if to impart the wisdom of Buddha: "It's nice to be nice."

Yep, it's nice to be nice and the email was a bouncy and very charmingly-extended invitation to go and meet Victoria Lopyreva, who is one of Russia's ambassadors for this tournament. She "made history by becoming the second woman in the world to kick the ball on the pitch to mark the beginning of a match: the first was Marilyn Monroe." That was news to me. That 2007 Women's World Cup I attended in China must have been one great, long hallucination. I must check with Anita Asante and Anna Kessel to see if they had the same dream.

Still, reading on in the email, Victoria is clearly a force to be reckoned with. She represents charities, champions refugees, promotes Russian tourism and is "bringing fashion and feminism into the football world". She has been awarded her country's "Medal for Brave Work" and is a "philanthropist at heart" who can also turn her hand "to help develop sporting infrastructures".

Vicks was Miss Russia in 2003 and, to be fair, there are easier titles to win. The email is from a PR company looking to hook her up with *The Sunday Times* and the suggestion is I interview her on that core mission, "bringing fashion and feminism to the football world". I have two daughters, a wife who loves football, and think anyone who doesn't support feminism should be cast on a desert island with Jeremy Clarkson, Donald Trump and Katie Hopkins (and on the island there'd be a giant billboard saying THIS IS WHAT YOU WANTED). I'm also rather pleased with the summer coat I bought for Russia so, bringing fashion and feminism to the football world ... me and V would have plenty in common.

But I don't think I'm going to do the interview because there's just too much great actual football to write about. Yesterday evening I was at Jorge Sampaoli's pre-match press conference and tonight I'm going to Argentina v Nigeria. It could be Lionel Messi's last World Cup game. Sampaoli cut a contradictory figure as he tried to bat away suggestions of a players' coup and instil confidence that "Argentina will turn a new page ... we have five games to win the World Cup and tomorrow must be the start". His words were defiant in theory but the way he delivered them was muted and troubled. Sampaoli is in danger of not just presiding over one of his country's greatest football embarrassments but hastening the end of the international career of perhaps the world's best player.

He admitted Nigeria will be fitter and faster than the side he is going to send out. He is going for an XI based on Messi's favoured 4-3-3 formation (having disastrously tried 3-4-3 v Croatia) and he is falling back on Argentina's "historical players". These are guys like Gonzalo Higuain, Javier Mascherano, Angel Di Maria, Ever Banega and of course Messi himself. They are the veterans of either Argentina's 2014 World Cup final or 2008 Olympic final, which they won against Nigeria. From these two high points in Argentina's recent football history Sampaoli is hoping inspiration will flow and carry his team past Nigeria's younger legs.

So I want to talk about World Cup casualties. Sampaoli is attracting ridicule for his Pitbull-meets-Simon-Cowell look. And for the confused and flawed job he has done with this Argentina team. But I feel for the guy. He is a very fine coach, with a fine record in South American club football, a very good stint at Sevilla behind him and of course the glory of leading Chile to a first Copa America on his CV. His Chile were one of my favourite teams at the last tournament. So it is sad that he now seems destined to go down as a figure of fun. All because of one bad month. But that is what the World Cup does. I have written that the level may not be as elevated, technically and tactically, as the top end of club football, but nothing compares to the pressure and the projection of World Cup games.

Messi, who is now 31 and hinting at international retirement, may end up slightly diminished, reputationally, because of World Cup travails. Sergio Aguero, the one "historical" player Sampaoli does not seem prepared to rely on, could quit Argentina too and like Messi his World Cup troubles will be held against him.

Egypt's failure will affect how Hector Cuper is regarded. Fabio Capello never had the same respect following 2010. Willy Caballero will never get over his howler v Croatia, just as Rob Green never lived down his mistake for England v USA in 2010. The beautiful, poignant, BBC documentary about Scotland's 1978 campaign details how that broke poor Ally MacLeod.

You could see Edinson Cavani's sheer relief when he scored for Uruguay yesterday. He knew if he went through the group phase without a goal the questions would start (especially with partner/rival Luis Suarez doing so well). Mesut Ozil being bombed out by Germany will cause more damage to his reputation than 50 limp performances for Arsenal. Gerard Pique has suddenly plummeted in the world defender rankings as a result of Spain's group phase.

All this is to emphasise the high stakes everyone is playing for here. The World Cup really does test people in a way no other competition can and that is why it is 'admissible evidence' when we have those 'Greatest Ever' debates (and why the answer to 'Messi or Ronaldo?' remains 'Pele').

Part of me hopes Messi and Sampaoli are reprieved tonight. But another part says hey, this is sport. And also, wouldn't it be great for African football if Nigeria (and Senegal) sweep through into the 16? Morocco have been one of the best teams at the tournament and are unlucky to be heading home with so little reward. But whatever the result, let's just remember things on a human level: hearts, dreams and reputations are being crushed out there at times. In those moments the participants deserve our sympathy.

Predictions today (they were dreadful yesterday so will attempt to do better here): Australia 1 Peru 0; Denmark 2 France 2; Argentina 3 Nigeria 1; Croatia 1 Iceland 1

Player to watch: Victor Moses (not really). Sampaoli said in his press conference yesterday that Nigeria have lots of great players that Argentina must fear, "like Moses". He couldn't name any others. But am I really saying Victor Moses is the player to watch today? Of course not. It's Messi

What happened next: Australia beat Peru but France and Denmark's mutually beneficial draw saw both teams through. Croatia beat Iceland, opening the door for a Messi-inspired Argentina to beat Nigeria 2-1 and progress. You're going to read all about how he did it over the page

— Day 14, June 27
Being There

I won't ever forget what I saw last night at the St Petersburg. Ever Banega's pass dropping out of the sky, Lionel Messi cushioning the ball while at the same time nudging it away from the defenders with one astonishing, improvised touch with his thigh. Then another magic touch, before the ball hit the ground, with the top of the toes of his left foot. And then the finish: the shot planted beyond the goalkeeper with what is supposed to be Messi's weak right foot. All done at top speed, his little legs whirring like a wind-up toy. I won't forget that. This is the second time, in terms of live football watching, that I've witnessed Messi perform a particular function of play with brilliance beyond anything else I've seen.

- Best pass I've ever witnessed: Messi to Di Maria, Brasilia, 2014
- Best first touch: Messi's 'thigh of God', St Petersburg, 2018

Someone asked me recently how many matches I think I've been to, ever. At a conservative estimate, as a full-time football reporter, I'd work at 65 games in a normal season. I've just finished my 23rd season as a full-timer. That's around 1500 games. At tournaments I'd see, on average, an additional 15 games. World Cup 2018 is my tenth tournament. So, add 150 games. Before being full-time I freelanced for a year and a half. Let's say another 50 games. Games seen as an Aberdeen supporter? My dad was very good at taking me every week (though let's not speak about him deciding against going to Gothenburg). From ages seven to 18. 25 games a season. Plus those in adult life (not nearly enough, having left Northeast Scotland almost 30 years ago). Call it another 300 games.

So, we're talking about 2000 matches. There are around 800-1000 passes in any game of football. Ergo, I've seen in the region of 1.8m passes, live. Messi's in 2014 was the best. Touches? I'm really extrapolating here, but Premier League stats suggest a median of around 600 touches per team, per game. Let's say I've seen around 3.2m touches, then. The Messi thigh is unsurpassed.

I'm trying to drill into all this because last night's experience in St Petersburg re-emphasised the unbeatable experience of watching games live. It's something you embrace as a football reporter and you have to argue your corner over it, time and again. The vast majority of people who read our stuff have not been in the stadium. They've experienced the game on television, by radio, via social media or not at all until reading our reports. Readers who take umbrage at what reporters write often trot out the old accusatory line "did you even watch the same match?" And, actually, the answer is no.

A TV viewer will see more than a live reporter, in some ways. They have HD, replays, commentary, punditry to inform them and can focus 100% on watching the game. Whereas inside the stadium you have no replays, no commentary and one pair of eyes compared to the 24 Super HD cameras Sky have at every Premier League game. You miss stuff. You don't fully see stuff. And there's a whole lot of other stuff in the stadium to take in.

Now imagine being a match reporter. Add to this already imperfect viewing experience a laptop screen in front of you and 1000 words to write *by full time*. You're seeing so little, in many ways, compared to the TV viewer. See those match ratings reporters give? Ever wondered why a seemingly useless player and seemingly important player got the same 6/10?

Trust me, don't waste an ounce of mental energy getting indignant about match ratings. We reporters are playing bingo. Clutching at straws. Watch 90 minutes of football while writing 1000 words and at the same time precisely and accurately rating 26 players? Forget it. Earlier in this trip I had a conversation, in a check-in queue, with Martin Samuel, a doyen of our business, about match ratings. Martin told me of a trick he'd learned from one of the old journalists, which is to accept that if you see any player in two clear moments in a match, while everything else is going on, you're doing pretty well. So, if first time you see someone play the ball they do something good ... 7/10. They f*** it up ... 5/10. Next touch is good, give them another mark. Bad, subtract a mark. Can't remember seeing them at all? 6/10 is safe. Iffy as it may sound, I can tell you this is as logical a way of doing the marks as any other method I've heard of and if it's good enough for Martin, it's good enough for me.

Anyway I've digressed a bit from Messi but I was reflecting, today, on the experience of watching him live. I am by no means a Messi fanboy. There are areas where I'd go with Ronaldo in the eternal debate. But that's twice Messi has 'done me' live. And I think you really, truly, have to see football in the flesh to see it properly.

You don't appreciate the extraordinary speed of top football until you see it live. You don't feel the weight of shots and tackles. You don't get the sense of space and angles: how little room there is for a player to perform their skills, the picture of the whole pitch around them and how much they are trying to take in while executing an action.

And you are not immersed in that most indefinable but in many ways important aspect: the atmosphere in the stadium, the tension in the air, the importance of the particular moment, the pressure.

I wrote/gushed about Messi's goal for *The Times* and under the piece one reader has written "all a bit OTT" while another has said "I'm not convinced anyone would be going on about this goal if it hadn't been scored by Messi". I'm not bothered or surprised by these reactions because I've watched the goal back on television and it loses 50%. That's what these readers saw. But I saw the 100% version. I was there.

I saw the speed at which Messi operated. I watched him spend the previous 13 minutes lurking, loitering, peeling away, coming back in, continually trying to find the kind of space where he could be free and start a run like the one he made. I saw him set off on that run before anyone else on the pitch, even Banega, saw the play was possible. I saw his body position, the difficulty of keeping his balance, the incredible improvisation it took to come up with that magical touch with his thigh. I felt the breathless, heart-in-throat tension inside the stadium last night as 50,000 Argentinians had eyes fixed and hopes pinned on him. I know what I saw and let's say it was, in Aberdeen parlance, 'nae bad at a'. In fact my worry about my piece is not that it was OTT, it's that it didn't – couldn't – do Messi last night justice.

PS: Was sat between Sid Lowe and a Nigerian reporter in the press box. Sid is an absolutely brilliant writer on Spanish football. He probably attends 30-40 La Liga/Champions League/Copa Del Rey matches featuring Messi every season. So he has probably seen Messi live 500 times. And in Messi's finer moments last night, Sid was as excited, as blown away as if he were watching the little maestro for the very first time.

That told me a lot about this footballer's powers. The Nigerian reporter went through agony but he gave me a delicious moment. Before the game Nigeria's left-back, Bryan Idowu, ill-advisedly said he wanted "to make sure it will be Messi's last World Cup game". Idowu was the opponent Messi tormented more than any other in the first half (before the second, when Argentina became an utter mess and Messi went into his shell). At the worst point of the torture, the left-back was so spooked he sort of mentally gave up and just passed the ball straight to Messi. The Nigerian reporter started thunderously typing. Don't know if it was a tweet, a note for his match report or a message for his editor, but the words on his screen were simply: REMOVE IDOWU.

Predictions today: (Okay, so I had two hours sleep after getting back from the game before a day's travelling. Am in Kaliningrad now and had to sleep ... so it's half-time in the first games. I'm cheating a bit here): Germany 1 South Korea 1; Mexico 0 Sweden 1; Serbia 0 Brazil 2; Switzerland 2 Costa Rica 1

Player to watch: Alisson. It hasn't been a great World Cup for goalkeepers, confirming that this really is not a golden age for No.1s. Alisson has not been hugely tested yet but I'm watching him closely here, trying to gauge how good he really is

What happened next: South Korea won 2-0 to knock out the world champions. Sweden won 3-0 to top the group. Switzerland progressed with a 2-2 draw against Costa Rica; Brazil eased through with a 2-0 win in which Alisson continued to be underemployed. By the end of the summer, he would be at Liverpool as (briefly) the world's most expensive keeper

— *Day 15, June 28*
The Cut of a Jib

I think we've reached peak Gareth. Or have we? Back home, are there town centres full of blokes squeezed into skinny waistcoats, with well-groomed beards? According to Henry Winter this morning, England fans are set to unleash a new song at tonight's game. It's to the tune of *Whole Again* by Atomic Kitten and the words are:

> *Looking back on when we first met,*
> *I cannot escape and I cannot forget.*
> *Southgate, you're the one, you still turn me on*
> *And football's coming home again.*

Wow.

Leaving aside what a taste for 20-year-old Atomic Kitten numbers tells you about England fans in terms of demographic (they're not reworking J Hus or Migos, that's all I'm saying), just consider for a moment where the country's relationship with the England manager has got to. It was not long ago that Gareth was being dismissed as 'safe' and 'boring' and 'Mr Nice'. Old-school fans wanted a Real Football Man in charge. 'Arry in the dugout, and Pride In The Shirt.

Hipsters wanted, actually, to support Peru, but if they had to suffer having an England team then their ideal candidate for manager was Someone Like Bielsa. Someone Like Bielsa is pretty much the hipsters' choice for any job.

Gareth? To one side, 'not enough pashon', to the other, too English, too FA. But now? Suddenly England is Germany in 2006: a young, likeable team with a fresh spirit and refreshing vibe, uniting fans of all generations and viewpoints. And a lot is down to Gareth himself. As someone tweeted, he's like the next-door neighbour you think is too straight-laced, but then one sunny day he surprises you by slipping a sly Estrella your way over the garden fence and from then on, he's all right, him.

I got to know Gareth a tiny bit, socially, around the 2010 World Cup when he was writing a *Sunday Times* column. He vibsed (her word) with my missus in the bar after a *Times Plus* event, he came to South Africa to cover the tournament for TV and would meet David Walsh, the chief sports writer at the *Sunday Times*, with me tagging along, for the odd meal in a shopping mall in Johannesburg.

He's very much an ordinary guy, quietly funny, self-deprecating, no ego, open, empathetic, a bit of an anti-star, an antidote to Big Timery. So now that the country has got to know him, I'm not surprised how much he is liked. He's the version of England and Englishmen the wider world likes.

Still, "Southgate ... you still turn me on." Just, wow.

Anyway, I've been thinking about how Gareth comes across and how important image and persona has become in football management. I think Jose Mourinho started it, by swaggering into English football with good looks, youth, a bit of sartorial style (we're talking 2004 and long before the day he became the middle-aged guy who bought the Adidas shop). He was so different to older managers around in the Premier League at the time and so successful that he established an idea that managers had to be, more than successful, cool.

They had to look the part, walk the walk and Pep Guardiola, dressed like an Apple exec, is another who has a style and look that furthers their brand. Jurgen Klopp cultivates the big smile and lovable eccentricity a bit: Klopp knows people love it, knows what he's doing. Poch succeeds in looking just how he wants to be as a manager: like the big brother of the players. Thinking back, the top managers always had ways of looking, dressing, behaving that enhanced their myths, helped their success by getting inside their own fans/players' heads, but also those of rivals. Fergie visually projected 'tough, intelligent, street-wise Scot'. Not for nothing did a columnist in the *Manchester Evening News* dub him 'Sir Taggart'.

Wenger was the sophisticated, bookish Frenchman when he arrived. Go back to Shankly, Clough, Stein and see how powerful image was to them. And Gareth Southgate is so popular at the moment because he just comes across as what most British blokes would like to be, or grow into, or have for a son-in-law. He still looks athletic, he can dress himself, there's an intelligence about how he projects himself but also a down-to-earth quality. And of course results are good, so what's not to like? I think this is the first time I've covered England where the manager, rather than any of the players, has been the star.

Visuals? Well you looked at Joachim Low last night and saw the t-shirt and jeans and a guy not growing old gracefully. You look at Jorge Sampaoli and see something similar, Popeye-meets-Pitbull: shirt too young, too tight, and – *eeek*! – those tattoos.

But it's interesting. Look at pics of Sampaoli when he was winning Copa Americas with Chile and being lauded around the world. He had the same look then, it's just nobody was talking about it. Same with Low when he was winning the World Cup with Germany. He hasn't changed, just results and therefore perceptions of him.

When you're winning you can get away with anything.

Well, nearly anything. I mean, Atomic Kitten? Southgate you turn me on?

Predictions today: Senegal 2 Colombia 2; Japan 1 Poland 1; England 0 Belgium 0; Tunisia 3 Panama 2

Player to watch: Takashi Inui interested me when I watched Japan's last game. Clever, skilful, hard-working. I must confess I didn't know much about him until then but he has had a decent career, doing well in the Bundesliga, then for Eibar. At 30, and having just signed for Betis, he probably won't be coming to the Premier League at any point but he looks like the kind of footballer who would have been a good signing for Bournemouth or Fulham were he at a different stage of his career

What happened next: Colombia and Japan progressed to the knockouts with 1-0 wins – Japan having appeared to settle for a 1-0 defeat by Poland on the way. Belgium won the battle of the B-teams and Tunisia got the win their play deserved. Inui won a lot of fans in Russia, scoring two goals and leading Japan's creative play before starting his new chapter with Betis

— Day 16, June 29
Outcomes

Well, that didn't take long did it? 24 hours on from being the one, and turning people on, and all of that, Gareth Southgate is in a place every England manager visits sooner or later. The stocks. 'Momentum LOST Feelgood Factor LOST Game LOST' thunders the *Daily Mail*.

The *Daily Mail* doesn't muck about. Their sports coverage is quite exceptional, but there's a reason they are the paper that, above all others, people in the game want to stay on the right side of. Other papers and pundits are also unhappy. The idea of Southgate playing his 'B' side in order to rest stars did not sit well, instinctively, with a lot of us here and nor with people back home, it seems. And *The Mail* & co are reflecting that with their customary full force.

There are other, underlying reasons for the sudden infusion of negativity into the coverage. I'm writing this from Kaliningrad airport where we're waiting for yet another flight and there are a lot of blank eyes and hangdog faces. Very little chat or laughter. Steve Bates of *The People*, who I love to bits for his bright-and-breeziness, is still bright and breezy, but among the rest of us sparkle is in short supply.

I had a snooze in the Kaliningrad Stadium media centre yesterday, at my desk. Lovely it was. We're at that stage of the trip. Fatigue has well and truly set in and, mentally, it's a difficult point: it's 17 days since we left Britain, a long time to be away from home, and yet there is still a fair way to go. Another 17 days before our return flights to London. We miss home, miss our kids, miss our wives, miss our own beds, miss switching off. The fact that it's currently sunny back in England, and our friends and loved ones are gearing up for the weekend, is difficult too: you look round another grey airport lounge and think how you'd rather be in the garden. Some are annoyed at missing stories. Some don't think the FA are giving us enough access. Some would rather there was a little *less* organised FA stuff, so they could do more of their own off-diary things. Last night, I'm told, one writer asked another to step outside.

At times like these I have to also remember that, while England aren't my team, England is *the* team for a lot of colleagues. They're England fans and they're going to be as disappointed as any supporters will be when a performance isn't good. And last night's England were certainly not good.

Finally, there has been so much positive coverage, and we've all been part of it, that there is a natural urge to balance the narrative. Journalists are professional sceptics, doubting is in our DNA so the first bad performance was always going to make some want to stop being so nice and start raising questions about the team.

So there are a lot of reasons behind the mood-change. You watch, there'll be more negativity tomorrow, but then in the run-up to England's next game, Colombia, we'll have had some sleep, had a weekend, we'll be in the final fortnight of the trip, excitement and hope about the team's prospects will rise again ... and the tone will change once more. I think, as an industry, we have to be careful about consistency at times like these. Something you pick up from social media is how much the public hates the 'build 'em up then knock 'em down' tendency they associate with the press. But in our defence: we are reporting on football and have you ever noticed those numbers beside a team's name on the results page or league table? We're in an outcomes-driven business. We report on protagonists that are forever being measured and those measures change game-to-game, week to week. We're not art critics, nor at the opera. There are no such things as masterpieces in football because masterpieces live forever, whereas one football match is always quickly followed by another and what we see a player or team do in one game can be made less relevant or valuable by the next. Messi's goal against Nigeria will just be a rather beautiful little footnote if Argentina now go out to France. Ronaldo's exploits v Spain have already receded because he was average in his next two games.

Sports writers have to keep changing tack because the performers do. To some extent, it's the teams and the players themselves who build up their statuses then knock those down. One of the old Glasgow press box stories is of a great Scottish football writer reporting on Scotland v Italy. These were the days when reporters ad-libbed their reports down the phone to copytakers: just dictated them off the tops of their heads. This guy was on deadline and Scotland were winning 1-0 in the final minute. He was giving the copytaker the intro to his piece and his voice boomed: "Magnifico! Magnifico! Magnifico!" But then, mid-sentence, Italy equalised. "Correction!" he barked down the line. "Scotland, this won't do!" From "magnifico" to "this won't do" in the space of seconds ... that sums up football reporting and, unless they change the scoring system, and award victories on points *a la* boxing, how can we ever get away from that?

Another tale. Think back to the 1999 Champions League final and Manchester United being outplayed by Bayern Munich for 90 minutes, with a team selection (the midfield) that didn't work, with Carsten Jancker hitting the bar at 1-0 ... and then United turning it all around in injury time. The following morning, reporters visiting Fergie at the United hotel toasted him with champagne. "Aye," said

Fergie with a smile but that glare in his eye. "Just remember, I read your first edition reports."

The hardest match report I've ever written was Wigan v Arsenal in an FA Cup semi-final a few years ago. Going into the game, Arsene Wenger was on the brink. Arsenal were without a trophy in several years, his contract was up for renewal and he was up against Wigan. The semi went all the way to extra-time and penalties. What made it so difficult was how extremely the narrative depended on the result. Win, and the story was Wenger marching towards redemption in the final. Lose and it was Wenger: The End. With nothing in between.

I'd imagine reporting on the match against QPR, where Man City won the 2011-12 title, thanks to Aguero in stoppage time, was equally hard. Mourinho is a manager who stakes so much on the result that it can be hard reporting about him. United's backs-to-the-wall 2-1 victory over Liverpool at Old Trafford last season was a 'Mourinho Masterclass' in many papers, but Liverpool so nearly equalised in the closing stages. If they had, the story would have completely changed, to being about how, via their manager's caution, United had blown a 2-0 lead.

Fans are outcomes-driven too. One of the worst games of football, and most anti-climactic Aberdeen performances I've sat through, was our Scottish League Cup final victory over Inverness Caledonian Thistle, 0-0, on penalties. Utterly grim until the shoot-out ended in our favour. I went away jubilant, celebrating with 50,000 other Dandies, but one missed penalty, and the shoot-out going the other way, would have had us cursing and calling for the manager's head.

So, don't blame football reporters if, to some extent, our judgments seem to change game to game. We can't avoid being swayed by outcomes. I think what we've got to try to do is look at underlying things, tactics, preparation, a team's culture, a player's journey, mentality, technique. That's what the best managers do. Guardiola, for example, is a fierce winner, but what he focuses on with his players is the process, the principles, the bigger picture.

When you understand sport in those terms, outcomes seem less random. United in 1999? Within that single match they got lucky but within the context of what Fergie created, the mindset he instilled in teams to never accept defeat and to always keep going for it, those stoppage-time goals were entirely logical.

Similarly, Istanbul was in one way inexplicable, but in another quite easy to understand, a consequence of something seen on many occasions, Steven Gerrard's unbelievable will. The way to make sense of Chelsea upsetting Bayern at the end of the 2012 Champions League final is through Didier Drogba: everything about the competitor he was, the journey he had, was expressed in that game. Man City may have needed the Agueroooo moment, but it arrived not randomly but because of the quality and mentality they'd been building over several seasons.

Of course, it is absurd to put Southgate on a pedestal then kick him off it because his B team lost, but I don't think the reporting today is really about that. He hasn't changed, nor have England's culture or tactics. It is just that we're early in the process of finding out how successful they really are. Simple fact: if England lose to Colombia, it becomes a disappointing World Cup. If England beat Colombia, it will be a successful tournament. That's how the nation will see it and the press are no different.

Last night? The issue isn't picking your B players. I think nearly every World Cup manager would have done the same. The questions we should be asking, as a media, are:

- Why was the performance so bad (B players or not)?
- Why was Southgate unable to change things?
- Is the squad balanced? Last night had me wondering why, for example, Danny Welbeck is here
- Have we been given a glimpse of England's true standing at this tournament? After all, several of those Belgium B players would be in England's first team. Moussa Dembele, Youri Tielemans for sure
- Did we see weaknesses in England's system (the way Belgium were able to overload the area in front of England's back three, which is being defended in Southgate's 3-5-2 by a single pivot)?
- Will morale be damaged?

Magnifico? Or, Gareth this won't do? The line will be a thin one in our reporting from here and that is natural. We, the football press, can't get away from being outcomes-led. But we do have to remember to ask the right questions.

— Day 17, June 30
Repino Swansong

I'm going to keep it brief today because it is deadline day and I'm way behind. I have a big piece to finish on England and penalties (problem: England players take them far too quickly), another to write on Romelu Lukaku and two major ones to do involving Harry Kane.

Harry – Prince Harry of Sunday Newspapers, he should now be called – stopped and talked to us in the mixed zone in Kaliningrad on Thursday evening. A lovely lad, Harry. Even better than his goalscoring is the way he talks in headline-friendly slogans. I was about three seconds into relaying to my editor what he'd said when the ed broke off to shout "Jonny's got Harry! Front and spread!" If only it was always that simple. Next goal I score at Friday night fives at Madani School, Leicester, Harry is quite welcome to claim it.

Dele Alli is also due in the England media centre soon for a press conference. Be nice to think he'll want a darts rematch but I doubt it. Anyway, I have a new playing partner, a Russian 'security expert' called Alex, who is working with ITV. Alex is one of the friendliest, loveliest Russians I've met here, always smiling, always up for some oche time and full of restaurant recommendations. You just have to ignore how he looks like he could kill a bear with his hands.

Anyway, going to just do a quick bit on the football here. All of a sudden there's not much World Cup left. Only 16 games and one of those doesn't count because it's the third-place play-off. Of those remaining, who have been the best teams?

Here are my rankings...

- Belgium: a surprise, because the talent of their players was always obvious, but I didn't expect them to come together so well. B team was excellent v England on Thursday (I could watch Dembele and Tielemans all day), and Hazard and Lukaku in fantastic form. If De Bruyne starts firing too, and Kompany's comeback continues, they'll be very hard to beat
- Croatia: fabulous midfield, Modric is proving an exceptional captain and in Mandzukic and Lovren they have leaders at the back and front
- Brazil: without playing anything like their best, they've been efficient, dangerous, strong and excellent on the counter-attack. Neymar playing like a self-obsessed show pony, however. If he starts passing, they'll win the World Cup
- Uruguay: Suarez is inspired, as he always is in the national shirt and it was important Cavani got his goal against Russia. Great backs and the midfield functions well
- Switzerland: I called them "fodder" in a podcast before the tournament and compared their high world ranking to that of all those irrelevant eastern bloc tennis players who get to No.1 when Serena is on one of her sabbaticals only to get hammered in the actual grand slams. Another terrible prediction
- Sweden: apart from Uruguay, is there a country that punches more consistently above their weight at tournaments than Sweden? A Swedish friend was telling me how much their nation loves the current

team. Without Zlatan, it is ego-free and a group of humble workers, who don't half make themselves difficult to play against

- England: defeat by Belgium has reduced the optimism but we shouldn't just suddenly forget the brightness of the opening two games. Reliant on Kane and set-pieces but that might be enough for the semis

- Spain: I still expect them to reach the final, but I've been disappointed so far. Brilliant opening-game performance, without actually winning the match, then fairly dull. Superbly talented squad however, and should get better

- Mexico: very good against Germany and a superb counter-attacking side, but just don't score the goals their approach play merits

- France: as I expected, an anticlimax. Great squad but didn't think Deschamps knew what to do with it at the Euros and still think that now

- Portugal: when Ronaldo plays like he did in the opening match they can beat anyone. Unfortunately, as their next two games showed, it is impossible even for Ronaldo to play like that every time. They seem to be petering out

- Colombia: for all their fine players, have not really been potent and were a bit fortunate to beat Senegal. The potential is there for them to grow, however, and England should be cautious. Love the young Mina-Davinson combo at the back

- Russia: energy and emotion have carried them to fine performances in their first two games but sooner or later they will surely run out of gas

- Denmark: solid. A "sticky" team to play against,

says David Moyes. Eriksen brilliant and Delaney an emerging star, but ordinary apart from that
- Argentina: the sublime (Messi) and the ridiculous (the lack of organisation) all in one team. I might be wrong, but just can't see Messi continuing to save them
- Japan: sorry Japan, love the country, always had a soft spot for the team but they've overachieved by reaching the second round and can't see Belgium being troubled

Predictions today (I enjoyed having a day off from getting these wrong yesterday): France 2 Argentina 1; Uruguay 1 Portugal 0

Player to watch: Cristiano Ronaldo. Could be a great player's last World Cup game. Then again, CR7 will probably lock himself in his cryochamber for the next four years and still be there in Qatar, goal-hanging and belting his free-kicks

What happened next: France beat Argentina 4-3 in a stone-cold thriller that saw Kylian Mbappe take centre stage. Uruguay were 2-1 winners over Portugal and so Ronaldo, like Messi, headed home after the round of 16

— Day 18, July 1
Personal Connections

Something lovely happened after the England press conference yesterday. Another reporter, one of my best pals here, was outside the Cromwell Hotel which houses the England media centre. He was in the car park doing a video call with his son when Dele Alli came out to wait for his shuttle back to England's hotel. My mate's son was excited, so my mate went over and asked Dele if he wouldn't mind saying hello.

Dele not only took the phone and did that, but then chatted for a few minutes about the computer game *Fortnite*, a big favourite among the England squad, but also 11-year-olds like my friend's boy. "What's your favourite gun?" asked Dele. "What uniform do you have?" After Dele handed back the phone, the kid couldn't believe it: "Dad ... did that happen?!" It made both their days.

I'm telling you this because I think my pal will forever be rooting for Dele now, as a player. I will, too, because of our darts match and also because of what happened yesterday. It will add another layer to covering Tottenham next season and what I want to let people know about are the personal connections all reporters have with different managers, players and clubs, and how they affect coverage.

My club is Aberdeen. I found covering Aberdeen very difficult because of this. I was biased against them, more than for them. I felt I had to demonstrate to readers my objectivity by not giving my own team an easy ride. Also, Aberdeen were abjectly crap during my years working for Scottish papers (1995-2001), and I was just angry, as a supporter. In defeat, I would get stuck right into them, two-footed. I remember a hideous 7-1 mauling at Celtic Park where about two thirds of my report lacerated our inept players and comedy manager Ebbe Skovdahl. The last 200 words were basically "Meanwhile, Celtic scored seven goals". Terrible reporting, because as much as anything the vast majority of our readership would have been Old Firm fans and rather more interested in Henrik Larsson's latest hat-trick than Rashid Belabed's chronic lack of pace. And ability. And game intellig... sorry, there I go again.

My allegiance has helped me report in England, I feel, because it means I'm fairly neutral. Fairly ... not totally. That's because of the personal connections which influence what I see. I arrived in England with Alex Ferguson on my pedestal and generally wanted his Manchester United to do well. But then in 2004 I moved to Liverpool, loved the place, loved the people and the Mersey clubs got under my skin too, furthering affections developed when I first came to England and old contacts from Scotland, Walter Smith and Gary McAllister, welcomed me inside Everton and Liverpool respectively.

Then I got to know David Moyes, and to like Everton even more. Then Rafa Benitez landed at Anfield and gave me one of my most special experiences as a reporter, covering the 2004-05 journey to glory in Istanbul. Getting to know the likes of Carra, Gerrard and Xabi Alonso made that extra special. So suddenly I wanted Liverpool, Everton and United to succeed, which obviously is not a logical position. Wigan came up and their young press officer, a certain Matt McCann, was brilliant and opened the doors to the club. Bolton were friendly too. And then I developed a relationship with Arsenal through another fantastic press officer, Amanda Docherty. I got to know Theo Walcott and his family, and kept bumping into his lovely parents at the 2006

World Cup. That was the year I also started working with Martin Jol, ghostwriting his column, so suddenly I wanted both Arsenal and Tottenham to do well, too. Now I'm in Leicester and they are close to being my English team. I envisage taking my daughters there. Except that the missus bleeds Canaries yellow and we got engaged after a Norwich game at Carrow Road, so let's just say 'OTBC'. Yellows will know what I'm talking about. I could go on, but wanted to give you an idea of how it works for reporters, because we all have similar conflicts.

All that said, your biggest allegiance is usually to the story. And to getting away with it, in terms of your match report, for another week. So you can be in the absurd position of watching your own club 1-0 down in the 90th minute and be half-hoping they don't equalise, because it will wreck your intro and force a rewrite of the copy that you have already filed and are pleased about.

I don't think readers like the idea of us taking personal feelings into our reporting, and nor should they. We need to be as objective as possible. But it's hard. If I'm writing about Moyes, I'm always going to try to state his case because I know what his case is, and I know the hurdles and challenges that made, for example United almost an impossible job for him.

Now? If Dele Alli gets himself sent off (and he's the type who will from time to time) I just don't think I'm going to be as harsh on him in a report as I would have been before – because I'll be able to put a mistake in the wider context of who he is. I wanted Egypt to do well in this World Cup because I love Mo Salah and a trip to his home village, Nagrig, furthered my understanding of his story. My daughter has decided to support Uruguay, so watching them beat Portugal last night made me happy. Do I dislike Germany like we in the English media are supposed to? Of course not. I have some fine German press colleagues and have forged links at Bayern Munich over the years. And England? Here I am, a Scotsman covering the Auld Enemy, quite happy when they're doing well, because of knowing and liking Southgate and many of the players.

Without giving away trade secrets, within the English media I'd say the best-supported teams are (in this order): Liverpool, United, West Ham, Arsenal, Tottenham. So now you know why there's so much West Ham in a lot of papers. Also, why Liverpool and United are both more praised and criticised than other clubs. And why, when a player plays for any of the above teams then, yes, they are more likely to be written about as someone who should be playing for England.

Bias? Here's a challenge. Watch a match involving your team, but try to watch both teams equally, ie focus on what the opposition are doing as much as your side. Difficult eh? Now do that and give me 900 words on the whistle.

Predictions today: Spain 2 Russia 1; Croatia 3 Denmark 2

Player to watch: Thomas Delaney. Moyes mentioned him to me when we were doing our column this week and he has just signed for Borussia Dortmund, who don't often get their talent-spotting wrong. He had an excellent season at Werder Bremen in 2017-18 and is a bit of a Danish/American Lampard

What happened next: Spain could not crack Russian resistance after 120 minutes of trying and failed from the spot, too. Danijel Subasic of Croatia beat Kasper Schmeichel of Denmark three saves to two in the other shoot-out. Delaney – one of the Danes' big performers in the tournament – had been subbed off before the pens

— Day 19, July 2
Penalties

I was starting to think this World Cup was like Rasputin; that nothing could kill it. That the vibe of good football, and of something fresh happening to revive the old tournament was going to stay. I hope it will. I hope that yesterday was just a blip and not the beginning of the end.

Yet yesterday felt horribly familiar, much too much like the grey and pragmatic World Cups of 2014 and 2010. First, Spain v Russia, a match where the Spanish made more than 1000 passes, only about five of which (Iniesta's) went forward. And where Russia had so little interest in playing that one of their defenders, Vladimir Granat, was on the pitch for 75 minutes and made zero passes, while receiving just one pass. Granat got 6.36 out of 10 in the creditable *whoscored.com* ratings by the way.

Then we had Croatia v Denmark, the nice Croatians against the earnest Danes, producing a match that apart from the first five minutes and last five minutes was palatable without having the slightest bit of oomph. The football equivalent of non-alcoholic lager.

Both matches went to extra-time (and when did you last see interesting extra-time?) before, inevitably, progressing to penalties. Effing penalties. Four hours of resolution-free, mostly event-free football then a couple of 'beat the goalie' competitions. You were back in the purgatory of Brazil 2014 or South Africa 2010, and at least South Africa had vuvuzelas to drown out your inner scream.

So, penalties. A few thoughts that occurred watching yesterday's shoot-outs. David De Gea. David De Gea, right? Possibly the best goalkeeper in the world. Key strengths: his unbelievable reflexes and ability to use any part of his body to make unorthodox saves. These attributes allow him to face up opponents even when they're at close range, to stay on his feet until the very last moment and see where the ball is going so he can then jut out some part of himself to save it. Seldom seen a better keeper from six yards. So why, from 12 yards, did De Gea feel the need to just guess which way a kick was going and dive early? He of all keepers should be able to wait until the penalty is taken before moving and then get near it. Yet De Gea kept guessing, diving, and getting beaten down the middle.

Laws of the game. *The Daily Mail* have done a good job on this today. Igor Akinfeev, Kasper Schmeichel and Danijel Subasic, the goalies who made saves in shoot-outs, were all leaving their lines. Yet no action was taken. No action, it seems, is ever taken when goalies break this law. *The Mail* counted that with 15 of the 19 penalties faced yesterday, the keeper illegally, but without punishment, left their line.

If there is one player on the whole planet who I'd back to score a penalty under pressure it is Sergio Ramos. Big, bad Sergio. A man who'd eat a kitten if that meant winning. A story via an assistant of Rafa Benitez: when Rafa was Real Madrid manager, early in the season, he felt Ramos was taking it easy in training, and so the manager tackled his centre-back. "Don't worry," Ramos shrugged. "I'll be ready in April." April being the business end. Anyway, yep, Ramos took a kick in Spain's shoot-out and scored.

Don't think I've ever seen a better goalkeeping performance in defeat than Kasper Schmeichel's. To save three penalties yet lose? Cruel.

A few thoughts about penalties generally...

Post-rationalisation: Surely penalties offer the greatest

evidence of how we post-rationalise things as reporters. When do you see reports about the team who "won undeservedly on penalties"? Not very often. You do see pieces about sides being undeserved *losers* after the *dreaded shoot-out*. But the story seldom gets written the other way. For example, Russia's penalties win is being reported as just punishment to Spain for their sterile possession play. Almost as an inevitable consequence of the 120 minutes of play that preceded it. But the very essence/problem of penalty shoot-outs is that they don't reflect very much other than the abilities of ten (or more/fewer) individual takers to handle, technically and psychologically, a static, single-action task. That's why, to use a bad cliche, they're a lottery.

We use them far too much to confirm a narrative we want to follow. Two instances would be the 2006 World Cup final and 2008 Champions League final. I was at both games. Both were incredibly taut and even contests, where good teams, competing heroically, just could not be separated. Italy won on pens in 2006 and the triumph was portrayed as an epic act of classic Italian football endurance; Fabio Cannavaro got the Ballon d'Or. But France were equally deserving on that night in Berlin. Had they won on pens we'd have written a different story, of their incredible resilience in the face of Zidane's red card and the character of a generation who prevailed despite being written-off as past it coming into the finals. Zidane or Thierry Henry might have won the Ballon. Should one solitary kick from 12 yards (France's Trezeguet was the only player to miss a penalty in the shoot-out) have made that much difference to the narrative?

Likewise, Manchester United's 2008 Champions League win was written as confirmation of Alex Ferguson and Cristiano Ronaldo's genius (and, by the way, I fully bow to both). But if Chelsea had won the shoot-out, wouldn't Fergie have been absolutely castigated (for a meagre European Cup record) and Ronaldo been the villain (he missed in the shoot-out)? And those penalties came down to the width of a post and John Terry slipping.

Another thing about penalties: rubbish as they are, they are still the best way of deciding things. This morning, as many times before, I sat trying to think of alternatives. Golden goal? Leads to even more negativity. Decide it on a 'fair play' countback of cards? Too easy for gamesmanship to creep in.

The two best proposals I've heard are...

- Instead of pens, player v goalkeeper, with player starting with ball on halfway line and taking it one-on-one v the keeper
- In extra time, after every five minutes, remove a player from each side; with fewer and fewer players on the pitch it will become easier to score

The attractions of these are that more skill and 'football' will end up deciding the outcome than a simple penalty shoot-out. I think they did the one-on-one thing in the US for a time. But I'd ultimately be against either being introduced. The reason? At least penalties are a part of the game, an action already used under the rules for deciding situations outside of open play. Shoot-outs are not great, but logical. Whereas the two proposals discussed would involve introducing new, contrived things into our lovably simple game.

Finally, I wrote a fair bit about England and penalties over the weekend. This meant speaking to experts, going back over tapes and reading the research out there on pens. Some interesting points (in case you missed these in the papers):

- Going first in a shoot-out offers a much greater chance of winning, statistically
- It's much easier to convert a penalty to win a shoot-out than it is to convert one to avoid your team losing. 92% of the first sort get scored but only 60% when players are in the counter-situation
- Research shows a team's best takers should go first and fourth
- If you celebrate scoring a penalty vividly, raising your arms above your head etc, the oppo's next taker is much *more* likely to miss
- England players take their kicks far too quickly, starting their run-ups an average of just 0.28 seconds after the ref's whistle. That's almost a sprinter leaving the blocks. Takers from every other country take more time
- 'Higher status' players are more at risk of missing. Think of all the stars who miss in shoot-outs. Maybe there's a reason. The academic considered the world's leading expert on shoot-out is a Norwegian, Geir Jordet, who discovered that players taking penalties after winning a Ballon D'Or or FIFA Player of the Year were statistically more likely to miss. "When high levels of egotism are threatened, emotional distress is triggered," Jordet wrote

*Non-alcoholic beer. That's going to be my pleasure/fate tonight. Another late evening yesterday, in St Petersburg, followed by an early morning train to Moscow. Very quiet press party in carriage No.2, me included. Need to conserve energy/health and get a bit 'new school' at least for a day. England tomorrow, a late night and then 6am train back to St Petersburg booked in case England lose and there is an 'exit press conference' in Repino.

Predictions today: Brazil 2 Mexico 1; Belgium 3 Japan 0

Player to watch: Kevin De Bruyne. While Hazard and Lukaku have been right at the top of their games, KDB hasn't reached the sublime heights of which he's capable. I'm wondering whether he's tired, whether it's the role he's asked to play by Martinez (in a midfield two) or whether there's only room for one leader of Belgium's creative play and that's Hazard. Or whether it's just a blip and we'll see KDB's quality from now

What happened next: Brazil never looked like losing to Mexico, but the same couldn't be said of Belgium, who were 2-0 down to Japan with 21 minutes left before the supporting cast of Vertonghen, Fellaini and Chadli stepped up – the latter finishing a wonderful move with De Bruyne, decisively, at its heart

I'm not sure if I told you earlier about being out with old mates from the Scottish press, in Rio, on the night England exited the 2014 World Cup. The most ludicrous of all England World Cup embarrassments: out after two games and six days, out (to borrow Henry Winter's line) before the players had finished their course of malaria tablets. Me and the Scottish reporters were in a bar talking about this latest of 30+ years of hurt. "Ah, England," sighed one of the lads, taking a satisfied slurp of Brahama. "They never let you down."

But strange things are happening in Russia. Not only do England have a side that just might not make a complete Boris Johnson of this tournament – they have a side for which, even if it fails versus Colombia this evening, it will be very hard to feel anything other than sympathy. It's not just Gareth Southgate's appeal, it's the whole 2018 England production: a really good, young, honest, humble bunch of players; a down-to-earth and realistic FA (at last!); fans perfectly behaved; a press that I believe has become one of the most outward-looking and proportionate around.

Maybe I'm biased when it comes to this last remark. But I look at the papers this morning: yeah, Harry Kane draped in a St George's flag, but with his benign, rose-cheeked, crescent-moon face smiling as he shouts. I see detailed and quality analyses of the Colombians, I see scene-setting English pieces that are very careful to put this game in the context of England having a fortunate draw and no right, because of past failures, to any arrogant assumptions. I hear conversations around the hotel and press bus that err on the side of caution, the lads paying great respect to Colombia's threats and keen to demonstrate awareness of England's flaws. It feels like English reporters talking up England has become a taboo. And the closest thing to jingoism in today's papers is *The Sun* sending a reporter to Santa Marta to place a St George flag on a statue of Carlos Valderrama. It's not long ago (the 2010 World Cup) that we had headlines like "Roo: I'll Blitz Fritz" (Fritz, of course, won 4-1).

We were talking at dinner last night about the famous Graham Taylor documentary, *The Impossible Job*. A number of my old press colleagues (hi Joe, hello Shep) feature in the press scenes and what's striking is how Taylor feels the need to try to motivate and man-manage the reporters in the same way as his players. "Get yourself up man, put a smile on your face, we're here for business!"

It was if the whole travelling England party: press, manager, team, the blazers, were on some joint patriotic mission. That was the vibe I picked up as a young journo, sent to report on the England camp during Euro 96: alpha males on the pitch, alpha males in the press room. 'Jings, this is all a bit hardcore,' I thought. This is what other nationalities, we Scots included, picked up about Eng-er-lund and in case we were in any doubt, their fans would chip in with their songs about the war or about colonial glory. And then there was their penchant for wrecking foreign town squares.

There's something intensely poignant about the Taylor film. It's the 'last days of Empire' feeling. This nice, decent but old-fashioned Englishman is adrift in a changing world, where even the bloody Norwegians won't just lie down and take their 3-0 beating – in fact they'll beat you – and where the Poles don't know their place and nor do the Dutch. Where even San Marino will come to Wembley and score.

"Can we not knock it?" Taylor famously beseeches in his dugout as a pass along the floor goes astray. Can we not knock it? Damn the world for changing. Damn football for becoming a more sophisticated business than a good old John Bull smash up to Big Les Ferdinand's head, or a channel ball to Andy Sinton. Near the end, when England are losing to Holland in Rotterdam and the end is nigh for their chances of qualifying for the 1994 World Cup, Taylor taps the lineman's elbow: "Referee's got me the sack, thank him ever so much for me, won't you?" You can't get more English than that.

But this England seem light years away from those days. They've come to Russia not to plant the flag, but bring their *Fortnite* dances, inflatable unicorns and 'new male' opening-up to the international party. Yet they're also here, as Ashley Young was saying at last night's press conference, to sing their national anthem with pride. *This* England we get, we allow, we like, us non-Englishman (or in my case, part-Englishmen). My colleague, David Walsh, wrote a lovely piece in *The Sunday Times* about Southgate and his desire to not just create a new type of England football team but do his bit for a new brand of English identity. "We have the chance to affect something bigger than ourselves. We are a team with our diversity and our youth that represent modern England. In England we have spent a bit of time being a bit lost about what our modern identity is. I think as a team we represent that modern identity and hopefully people can connect with us," says Gareth.

You listen to Southgate and feel that *finally* someone in the public sphere actually gets the England we all live in. I've experienced, since coming south of the border to live in 2002, how diverse and subtle and multiple modern Englishness really is. I've lived in Liverpool, where it's fair to say the identity is Scouse first and English a very distant second. I'm now in Leicester, friends with British Asians whose Britain is both the same and yet completely different to mine. And I look at my daughters, with their Scottish names and English accents, their mixed-race beauty and millennial citizen-of-the-world future. Suddenly it feels England have a team capable of playing for all of that. I'll be let down, actually, if they go out.

PS: Thankfully Sunday *was* a blip. Yesterday the World Cup rose back up, like Rasputin from the ice, and produced one madly brilliant game (Belgium 3 Japan 2) and one contest of high football class (Brazil 2 Mexico 0). There are only ten games left in this tournament and it is on course to be the best since 1986.

PPS: We (the press) do a sweepstake for every England game. Last time, only one person bet on a Belgium victory and scooped the pot. This time there is a lot of money on Colombia, but I've gone 1-0 England (Kane, 15). Mind you, you now know what my predictions are like.

Predictions today: Sweden 1 Switzerland 1 (Switzerland 2-1 in extra-time); England 1 Colombia 0

Player to watch: Harry Kane. It truly does depend on him. Don't actually think he has played that well so far, in an all-round sense, and yet he is the tournament's leading scorer. Guess that sums him up

What happened next: Harry Kane scored his last goal of the competition – from the spot – and also converted in the shoot-out England needed to get by a gnarly Colombia side. Sweden edged out Switzerland with the only goal as the Three Lions' path to the final appeared to open up

— Day 21, July 4
The Difference Between Us and Them

I'll never forget my first live boxing. It was a bill at the Kelvin Hall in Glasgow and I was reporting for *Scotland on Sunday*. I can't remember who fought in the main bout. Perhaps Barry Hughes, maybe Scott Harrison. What I do remember is what jumped back into my mind at the Spartak Stadium last night: the sound. The thwack, thwack, oooff; thwack, oooff.

You've watched boxing on the telly, right? Apart from the denouements, when there is a knockout or stoppage and the fighting is scrambled, the violence unmistakable, for the most part the action appears measured, strategic, even tame. The fighters are feeling each other out, avoiding trouble and landing punches of seemingly limited venom. Then you go sit ringside at an actual fight.

Thwack, thwack, oooff. Close up you hear the damage, the impact of glove upon flesh, the force with which blows are being driven into the opponent's body. Each one sounds like it could knock you over. And then there are the other sensations. The welts and bruises you see coming up on the fighters' skin right in front of you. On TV these don't really show but from ten yards away, after a round or two, the fighters look like they've been birched.

Sweat, snot and sometimes blood flies your way at ringside. You start to properly get the footwork, the speed at which these guys are moving. You gain a sense of the supreme fitness effort involved to box even one round. And the sounds of those blows keep coming. Sounds daft, I know, but I remember thinking to myself at that very first bout: 'My god. They're really *hitting* each other.'

All of this came back to mind in the Spartak Stadium last night. It was a treat of a game. The tight, even, no-quarter-given contests are the ones I enjoy most and our press seats were closer to the pitch than normal, just ten or 12 rows up. Close enough for an unusually intimate view of the players. You could see how very little space anyone had because of the speed and ferocious workrate of both teams; how quickly gaps got filled and passing lanes were being closed off. On the Colombia side, you could observe the power, the muscle, the stupendous will and concentration of Yerry Mina. For England, the way Harry Kane was buffeted by challenges and Raheem Sterling was forever being surrounded and hounded, enabled you to understand how difficult life was made for them.

But mostly it was the sound. The penalty shoot-out took place right in front of us. We weren't far off being level with the spot and the noises of those players striking the ball will reverberate with me for a long, long time. Kane: that jiggling little run-up and then *bam*. Marcus Rashford, up to the ball, *blat*. Kieran Trippier, straightforward and nerveless Trippier, a simple run-up then ... *crack*.

These were the noises of hard, clean, violent impact; sledgehammers on masonry, axes laying into wood. These were not sounds you hear when balls are struck at the levels of football ordinary people play. And it was the context: unbearable tension, long preamble, but then the absolute explosive surety of the ball-striking. What you were hearing was technique.

And that's the thing. We look at sportspeople and kid ourselves we could almost be them if we were a little taller, a little younger, had a bit more fitness, a bit more luck. We talk a lot about their characters, their stories, journeys, the coaching they receive. All relevant but you know what? We lack their technique. End of story. We could never acquire it in a million years. Yes, Kane is an incredible tale of sacrifice and mindset – the kid discarded by Arsenal, encouraged by his dad to just get on with it and who fought off that initial disappointment to win another chance at Spurs. The youth who came through moderate loan spells and drifting development years, to still push himself to the top. The man who is so fanatically professional that he has his own chef and a house next to Tottenham's practice ground where he stays during the week so he can be 100% focused on training, while his wife and kid are in the family home in Essex.

None of that's normal but sacrifice, hard work, doing whatever it takes? We're all on *that* spectrum. It is not too big a stretch for any of us to imagine dedicating ourselves if we had a one-in-a-million career chance like Kane's. We could get the mental coaching to handle the pressure moments. We could show courage in battle and display dressing room good-eggery. These things about sports people that we can relate to are what we praise. But then there's the other stuff. The bottom line is that normos like us could strive like the pros, build ourselves physically and mentally like the pros, even acquire similar coaching ... and we would still be lacking. For the dividing line between us and them is that invisible margin that so seldom gets talked about.

Technique.

That ball-striking in the Spartak? I could hit a football 10,000 times and never make it come off my foot with a sound so pure as they did. Not close, not once. Never could I hammer a shot into the exact spot 12 yards distant where I need it to land, never mind also with the speed needed to elude a 90-caps international keeper like David Ospina, when he's diving the right way. I reckon any of us, if we put enough time into it, could work at acquiring the mental tools required for a shoot-out situation and yet they'd be irrelevant. We just wouldn't have the technical ones to succeed.

Technique is the true dividing line between sport's elite and the rest of us. Think of the best golf shot you've ever hit, then think about hitting that quality of shot every single time you address a ball, only with more power, more spin, and greater strategy. Congratulations, you're now a low-level tour pro. You probably still don't have the technique to go any further. You think you've faced a quick delivery at cricket, and seen plenty on TV, then you go to a county match and realise that even moderate professional fast-bowling is so swift your naked eye can't see it. Same if you ever watch a professional tennis player serve.

Technique is the thing. Technique, even more than mental strength, is what gets an athlete through pressure situations. Three England penalties in the shoot-out were technically sublime. Kane, having scored high and centrally with a spot kick in normal time, knew he had to vary it and drilled a perfect shot into the corner. Trippier's penalty was a must-score for England and was the best of all, whipped into an unsaveable area, the top-left corner. And then Rashford, a kid, whose performances this season for club and country have sometimes suggested doubt has crept into his wonderful natural game. In the press box, as he began his walk from the halfway line, you thought … Marcus? But there was such certainty and purity in the shot he hammered hard and low. The *thwack* of his foot on ball made the most perfect sound of all.

Kane practises everything, practises until he's a footballing robot when it comes to technical matters. We've seen Trippier's set-pieces throughout the tournament and how much craft he has in his right foot when striking dead balls.

Rashford? I've got to know Paul McGuinness a little. Paul was an essential part of Manchester United's coaching team for almost three decades, an original thinker with a passion for challenging players in unusual ways that demand high technique. He coached Marcus from the ages of around 12 to 18. On Wednesday afternoons at Carrington he would set up a mass game in the gym hall, a free-for-all for young players of all ages, creating conditions akin to street football games. Marcus, at the age of 13, was put in against 17 and 18-year-olds like Paul Pogba and Ravel Morrison, on a small court. It took brilliant technique to survive against the bigger, older boys.

McGuinness did lots of one-to-one work with Rashford and found a youngster who loved learning and thinking about technical aspects, who in the evenings would excitedly text him during Champions League matches with things like 'see what David Villa did there? – it was like that turn you showed me'. Over the past couple of seasons we've seen Rashford emerge as a free-kick taker, with a bunted 'knuckleball' shot he has clearly spent hours practising at Carrington. He was able to take this skill to another level by scoring with his speciality shot from long range in England's warm-up versus Costa Rica.

He is a youngster with rare technique and technical work-ethic, and that's what we saw when he smashed his pen past Ospina. What separates us, the mortals, from them, the professionals most of all is not complicated but it is fundamental. It's technical. It's kicking a football so true the sound rings out like a sledgehammer.

PS: Really pushing the limits, sleep-wise, now. Returned from last night's game to hotel at 2am and then did a

Sunday Supplement podcast until 4am. Bed and then up at 5.30am for the train back to St Petersburg. Our carriage was quiet but every so often an English voice would croak "coming home". And John Cross can't stop grinning. I'm really pleased for the English lads and the England team, there is nothing like coming through a super-tight game. And the penalties hoodoo is gone. Colombia though: gang of pirates, bastardry with outbreaks of brilliance. It was like watching a classic Uruguay side of old and I have to say I secretly loved it: yet more flavour to the World Cup. Fabulous fans, too. And in Yerry Mina I think we're seeing the emergence of a future great.

PPS: I've banged on about the penalty takers but what about that Jordan Pickford save? Eye on the ball, use your reflexes. Were you watching, David De Gea?

— *Day 22, July 5*
Win/Lose scenarios

Back to Repino, today, for England's latest offering of talk, darts and all-round nicery to the press. It's sunny, people are bouyant and you can't help thinking how different it would have been had the shoot-out against Colombia gone the other way. The media centre at the Cromwell would be getting dismantled today. There would be photos of sombre hotel staff carting off the pool table and taking down the dart board. The tastefully subtle Three Lions signage would be out the back, in a skip.

Provisionally scheduled for yesterday was that England exit press conference, where Gareth Southgate would have been asked to justify yet another tournament failure. Make no mistake, all the sympathy and goodwill towards Gareth would not have saved him from an inquisition, and amid the follow-up today, there'd be a few articles posing the question as to whether he should keep his job.

As it is, England's victory means that even if they fail against Sweden, this World Cup will be seen as a good tournament, and Southgate and the FA as being on a positive path. If the dart board at the Cromwell has to come down on Sunday, it will be with regret (at missing a golden opportunity) but it won't be an angstful image or one destined to go down as yet another of English tournament folly.

For Sunday papers, Saturday's quarter-final is the result of results. The World Cup final is never played on a Saturday, nor the semi-finals, so a quarter-final is the biggest game we can ever get to do live. To have England in one, and with a kick-off that gives us plenty time to finesse our coverage, it doesn't get bigger. This'll be up there with Champions League finals as the biggest match report of my career.

Before then, the job is a familiar one: producing 'win/lose scenario' articles. This often happens for pivotal Saturday games: league deciders, Champions League finals, England tournament knockout matches, even FA Cup finals sometimes. The idea is that readers will want some analysis that goes beyond the live match reporting, that tries to contextualise what the particular result means.

Of course, this puts the writer in a slightly absurd position of having to write one piece saying 'X's victory was confirmation of all their great work and a personal triumph for Y'. And another saying 'X's inevitable disaster was on the cards because of the flaws in their work, and is a personal calamity for Y'. Well, perhaps not quite so stark, but you get the point: these are the crafted versions of the leap from 'Magnifico, magnifico, magnifico…' to 'Scotland this won't do'.

I had to do win/lose scenario stuff for Liverpool in Kiev: one piece charting how Jurgen Klopp had scaled the heights, another describing how he still has a long way to go. You file both to the paper and they insert whichever fits the result. Reactive journalism? Well, isn't most journalism? And these win/lose things are unavoidable, it's not as disingenuous as it sounds. Results demonstrate what point a team has reached in their – cough – journey, and as I've said in an earlier entry, it's not only reporters but supporters whose judgments depend heavily on score lines.

The trick with the win/lose scenario pieces and the way to keep them authentic is to identify the themes, the factors and the fundamentals that survive whatever outcome. With the Liverpool win/lose in Kiev, it was about producing two articles essentially making the same argument, just framing them differently. It was about Liverpool's progression under Klopp and bright future, so long as the coaching and recruitment practices that brought them to the final continued.

With England, it'll be similar. Whatever happens against the Swedes, this has been the best tournament England have had since, what, 2004? One where they finally became a team to enjoy once again. One where behind the scenes and around the margins they got a whole lot of stuff right. A 5-0 defeat featuring a hat-trick by "150-year-old tortoise" Ola Toivonen might, of course, test this thesis. But let's cross that bridge…

So, here in the media centre, Jack Butland has just beaten Nigel Adderley at darts and the coffee is as rank as ever. I'm not the only one with win/lose in mind. A few of the lads have their own personal win/lose scenarios. There is not a single reporter not loving being part of an England (here we go all *X Factor* again) *journey* that has, for once, not ended in some abject and ridiculous disaster, and instead is rolling on and on. But equally some were rather looking forward to going home at this stage. There are guys with young infants, who are missing precious weeks of their development. There are lads with family holidays planned. There are boys who have to go straight from the World Cup to Wimbledon or the golf and wouldn't mind a break.

They don't *want* England to lose, but can see very shiny silver linings if they do. Their win/lose scenarios are full of mixed feelings. The grim line being uttered is that England are going to keep us out here right to the end … but the end is going to be an irrelevant third-place play-off a week on Saturday. Could well happen, but there's a silver lining there, too. A Sunday World Cup final and no pressure on a Sunday journalist to glean and publish the England starting line-up.

— Day 23, July 6
Potemkin Nation

Yesterday evening, sipping German craft lager, in a Tex-Mex barbecue house, in Rubinshteyna, St Petersburg, I had one of those moments of which journalists must beware. The oak-smoked, salt-dried brisket was melting in my mouth. The lager was crisp. The table company was great. A screen in the restaurant was showing highlights of seemingly random Premier League games (Leicester v Tottenham 2017-18 followed by an antique Blackburn v Manchester United match).

Our fellow diners were a diverse-ish, young-ish, fairly international crowd and the urinal in a stall of the unisex toilets was sculpted from a metal beer keg. Rubinshteyna is a relaxed, young and stylish street of restaurants and bars. And St Petersburg itself is jaw-droppingly beautiful. And so I had The Moment. "Wow," I thought. "We got it wrong about Russia."

This morning common sense and old journalistic instincts have kicked back in. Stay Sceptical. That's our training. Sceptical needn't have to mean negative or cynical, but it does mean retaining perspective about whatever you see, and retaining the impulse to question it. Is that real? Why is it like that? What am I *not* seeing?

In today's *Times*, Matt Dickinson has an interview with Garry Kasparov, the exiled chess master and critic of the Putin regime. Kasparov says Russia has become a Potemkin nation for the duration of the tournament. Grigory Potemkin was the lover of Catherine the Great who had fake villages constructed by the roadside as Catherine travelled to the Crimea. The villages were portable and as soon as the Empress passed, they'd be disassembled and put up again further down the route. All she saw on her journey was an idealised version of Russian rural life.

So, Russia as a 'Potemkin nation' – what Kasparov means is that Vladimir Putin has sanitised his country for the duration of this tournament, getting criminals off the streets, hooligans under control, de-littering his cities and herding foreign visitors towards shiny new stadiums, through revamped train stations and airports. Therefore, what we're seeing is not the real Russia. For Putin the whole World Cup is one big exercise in propaganda and soft power.

Kasparov is probably right. He knows his country and its ruler. I don't. But – stay sceptical – you have to also remember the context of Kasparov's remarks. Kasparov was one of the loudest and most articulate opponents of a Putin World Cup, and so he *has* to stay critical of it. He would look very foolish if he suddenly acknowledged the tournament as a success. Also, Kasparov's focus is solely Russia. I think it's true: this place has been done up, we're seeing mostly only the nice bits; it is summer and the place is happy because a tournament is going on. I have no doubt that, at other times, and especially in the polluted cities and poor villages that we're not seeing, life can be grim. Especially for Russians who oppose their dictator and the apparatus of his regime.

But this is not unique. The last World Cup was in Brazil, at a time where the economy was collapsing, people were suffering in dire poverty, and the president was soon to be impeached for serious corruption. Yet the Brazilian government and FIFA colluded to give us a sunny dollop of *jogo bonita*. Hey, don't look at that drug-torn *favela*, look over here: there's Marta with Fuleco, the zany armadillo

World Cup mascot. I love South Africa, it's a beautiful, buzzing country, but it is also, effectively, a one-party state, with the dynastic ANC always in power. And so the dubious Jacob Zuma used the 2010 World Cup to shore up his popularity. Sepp Blatter, odious and ridiculous, also used that tournament to play PR and politics. He had dreams of a Nobel Peace Prize, and saw bringing Africa its first World Cup as one of the stepping stones to winning it. I'll never forget Blatter's panic at Soccer City when Mandela drove on the pitch on a golf cart before the World Cup final. For weeks, Blatter had been hounding South Africa's frail, nonagenarian father-of-the nation for a self- photo op and Mandela wasn't having that. He gave Blatter the slip and then found a personal way to appear before his people.

At both Brazil and South Africa, cities were cleaned up, criminals were locked away. Those countries were airbrushed too. This isn't, in any way, to minimise or justify Putin propagandising the 2018 finals. It's just to say that, at World Cups, this is what often goes on. And let's not even start on Qatar 2022.

Two other reasons to stay sceptical. One is Uncle Rupert. Yep, I didn't buy my nice dinner last night, Rupert Murdoch did, just as he's paying for my hotel rooms, taxis and flights. Journalists on expenses shouldn't fall into the trap of thinking they're living real life. Pay for any trip yourself, even if you have plenty money, and it's a different dynamic. That said, we are working here, and facing challenges, speaking to people and getting into situations tourists don't, so the experience is more real in other ways.

The other thing I try to remember is Two Tribes. No, not Frankie Goes to Hollywood (great track albeit, better than *Relax*) but what happened at 2002. Half the journalists were based in Japan for the tournament, the other half in South

Korea and we only came together when the Korean lot flew to Tokyo for the final. It was like two tribes meeting. The lads who'd been in Korea were adamant they'd seen the 'true World Cup', and were full of stories about the wonders of Busan, Seoul, Jeju, Suwon, and the fervour of the fans.

We, the Japan half, were incredulous: to us, watching on TV, the Korea part of the tournament had looked a slightly eerie, choreographed exercise in local mass-hysteria with dodgy refereeing and possibly-corrupted games. The 'true World Cup' had been in Japan, of course. Both halves had got carried away and we were all guilty of falling uncritically in love with the countries that hosted us. We had all lost perspective.

But is 'guilty' the right word? What's wrong with falling for a place you visit? Because what you're falling for is invariably the people, the buildings, the beauty, the vibe. What's wrong with me enjoying St Petersburg, or Nizhny, or Volgograd, or Moscow, and deciding they're much nicer than I imagined? Because it can't *all* be fake. Putin hasn't been bussing 'Potemkin Russians' into every restaurant, street, shop and stadium. There *are* lovely, friendly, switched-on, ordinary citizens here. Stay sceptical, stay very, very sceptical about the guy in charge of this country, but take away the age-old lesson that a people aren't necessarily like their leader.

Stories that journalists will come back with – like my colleague, David Walsh, leaving his laptop on a plane only for it to be handed in and presented to him by St Petersburg airport lost property – they're not all Potemkin experiences. My parents came to St Petersburg on holiday a few years ago, outside tournament time, and they have a similar tale, and had similar positive impressions to me.

And propaganda?

There are tens of thousands of South American fans here, completely unafraid to travel to Russia. Contrast that with the huge number from European nations who stayed away, and you realise that in our part of the world we get fed a different story about Russia than they do in other places. And this is the dilemma about FIFA, its historic corruption, the dictators it gets in bed with, its stunts pulled behind-the-scenes for certain places to win hosting rights. The net outcome can still be positive, the FIFA core mission still the right one: taking football and those who love football to all corners of the world.

Whether it be British journalists or Colombian supporters, Argentine ultras or Belgian TV crews, getting hundreds of thousands of us out to Russia and showing us Russians, and Russians us. Only good can come of that, surely? Just as it did when previous Afrophobic Europeans returned home in 2010 with a new awareness that in Johannesburg, Cape Town, Durban (maybe not weird old Bloemfontein) you'll find some of the best people in the world. You just have to stay aware of Putin, of Zuma, of Dilma, of FIFA, and separate out what you're experiencing.

I'm on flights, via Moscow, from St Petersburg to Samara. Now, Samara, a colleague told me, is "a shithole". It was once a closed city, the HQ of the Russian space programme, and the joke is that Samara is so awful that all Yuri Gagarin was trying to do when he went into orbit was get as far-the-hell away from Samara as possible. But I told this gag to Alex, the ITV Russian security man who I've been playing darts with at the media centre, and Alex looked blank. "Samara," he said, "is good. It has the most beautiful women in Russia." Different truths again.

Predictions today: France 2 Uruguay 1; Brazil 1 Belgium 1 (Brazil on penalties)

Player to watch: Kylian Mbappe. Sorry Ishbel (my eldest daughter has decided to be a Uruguay fan) but I think Mbappe will outgun Cavani. It is his time. He was absolutely sensational in the previous round v Argentina, and though Uruguay's defence is one of the best in the tournament, I'd back him to shine again

What happened next: Brazil outshot Belgium 27 to 9 but Belgium got out to a 2-0 lead and held out under huge pressure after the favourites got a goal back. France gave a lesson in game management in a 2-0 win over Cavani-less Uruguay. Mbappe would end the tournament as its poster boy

This is our World Cup final, the editor keeps reminding me, so greetings from Samara on the day of one of the biggest match reports I'll ever write. Samara is sunny but much cooler than a few days ago (25C compared to 36C on Tuesday). Alex, my Russian darts pal, was right. I like this place. The buildings aren't pretty but it has a waterfront along the Volga which was buzzing last night: fairground, nightclubs, and restaurants. In one of these we watched Belgium shock Brazil and Marouane Fellaini outplay Neymar. It has been that kind of World Cup.

Brazil's exit heightens further the sense of opportunity for England and excitement in newspaper offices. And therefore the sense of today being enormous from a Sunday newspaper point of view. I've been doing this for 23 years, but I do still get nervous about live reporting. Only occasionally, but I wouldn't be surprised if the stomach tightens at kick-off today.

For now, though, I'm pretty relaxed: having lunch at a place near our hotel where the playlist has veered from Carly Simon to Guns N' Roses and the clientele are similarly contradictory. I dropped my menu and the Russian at the next table picked it up and handed it back to me with a friendly smile. Nice bloke. Even if he had a biker's beard and camouflage trousers with a hunting knife strapped to his belt.

So, match reports. My dad (hello old boy) said I should write about them. Forgive me if you already know how they work, from a writing point of view, but for those who don't. When you write them depends on two things:

kick-off time and your outlet's production needs. Today I'm filing three reports. One for the first edition of the newspaper, the copy deadline for which is 6.30pm; the second a polished rewrite for later editions (9pm deadline) and the other one for online – this will be an 'on-the-whistle' match report, composed during the game and filed as soon as the match ends.

When you start doing them, even the shortest live report scares the bejaysus out of you. My very first were for an agency in Glasgow and the shortest were for Ceefax. Three sentences, summing up the game at full time. That was enough for butterflies. Later I began freelancing for papers like *Scotland on Sunday*, *Sunday Times Scotland* and the *Independent on Sunday*. Those were typically around 400-500 words. No laptops or mobiles in those days (yeah I'm old) and you dictated your report down a phone to a copy-taker, meaning you really had to start filing around 75 minutes to get done for full-time. I wrote my reports long-hand, though the older pros in the press box wrote theirs in shorthand or just ad-libbed.

An example: when England beat Scotland at Euro 96 I was on colour-piece duty and the moment Gazza's fluky, sorry, iconic goal hit Andy Goram's net, I had to sprint from the press box to find a payphone in one of the Wembley concourses and was still on to copy as the England fans streamed noisily past at the end of the game.

I used to try to lessen the stress by pre-writing chunks of my report: scene-setting paragraphs, maybe even the intro. The idea was to get 'words in the bank' but I don't find that a very satisfactory way of going about the job. We're there to report what we see, after all, not what we think before the game that we're going to see. With pre-written stuff you always end up attempting to fit the narrative to what you've already put down. So, these days, I just go in with a blank screen, albeit there are a couple of formulae you can use to make sure the words come easily, and the structure of the piece works.

My general rule is to watch the first 25-35 minutes as closely as possible. Get the formations, observe the patterns of play, ask questions like, 'What areas are a team attacking? What are their ploys? How are they using individual players?' I also look for who is 'on it' in terms of first touch, in terms of tackles and headers and, most of all, in terms of decision-making. The more football I watch, the more I believe decision-making is what defines good performances and great players.

After that it's a blur of multi-tasking. Watching while typing. Typing while watching. My missus asks how, given that in normal life I'm a prime example of how men can't do more than one thing at a time, I can suddenly become a top-class multi-tasker at my work. There is a simple answer to that and it's for the same reason that the islanders on St Kilda developed huge, cleft toes so they could climb the cliffs to find puffin eggs: the necessities of survival have deformed me this way.

To help structure, best to start with something easy like selection. "Raheem Sterling again played off Harry Kane, with Southgate deciding against bringing Marcus Rashford in, despite Rashford's form…" Then you're up and running. From a sentence like that, you can go into the action, beginning with the first involvement Kane or Sterling has. This "first chunk" of copy you write is actually for the middle section of the report.

Sometimes this has to be filed by the end of half-time, if deadlines are really tight and the sub-editors need to start working on it. Your second chunk (sometimes filed at 75 minutes) will be the 'tail' or the end of the report. The final chunk you write, the 'top', is your intro. What should an intro have? A sense of drama, pace and colour. A summing up of the game and what its outcomes mean. It should identify the main protagonists. It should flow naturally into your first chunk. It's most difficult to make all this hang together when a last-minute goal changes the result.

Today? I'm expecting a tight game. It's England v Sweden. Before kick-off I'll go and find the correct statistics, but I do know that the majority of their tournament meetings (and there have been plenty) have ended in draws. Sweden are a sticky side who Gareth Southgate expects to be highly awkward to play against. They have no stars, but they work their smorgasbords off for one another and, having seen them down the years, I know that they always set a certain 'par score' – they produce a level of professionalism and performance that any opponent has to beat in order to win the game.

This has done for Italy (in the play-offs) and for Mexico and Switzerland. England will have to hit the right standards, but I suspect that after something of an ordeal they'll come up with enough to win the game. There are worries about Southgate's team. Reliant on set-pieces, they don't produce many open-play chances and they lean heavily on Harry Kane. But they are the most collective of any England team I've reported on at a tournament, probably since '96, and relying on Kane and set-pieces is not so daft when both keep producing goals. Win and England will be in a semi-final, but that's on Wednesday and it will be the daily papers' territory. This is our World Cup final, today.

Predictions today: England 2 Sweden 1 (aet); Russia 0 Croatia 1

Player to watch: Marcus Berg. Swedish colleagues say he is much better than this World Cup has suggested – he is near the top of the rankings for unsuccessful goal attempts. An experienced second striker, who had a great record at Panathinaikos, the Swedes think it's only a matter of time before he scores and that it could be today. He, Forsberg and Olsson are the players to watch for England

What happened next: England could scarcely have dreamt of a more comfortable quarter-final against Sweden, for whom Marcus Berg ended the tournament with no goals from 15 shots inside the box. Croatia became the first team since Argentina in 1990 to win two shoot-outs at the same World Cup as Russia's run came to an end

I'm back in St Petersburg, in a coffee shop by the water, unsure whether the flat white, egg sandwich and *syrniki* I've just ingested was breakfast, lunch or dinner. It's 3.30pm here but what does that mean? We flew back from Samara by charter plane at 3am and were served hot meals at 4am. Before that, there was a media centre meal at 11pm. It's all very disorientating – like England being in the semi-finals of the World Cup.

So, the match report wasn't entirely successful yesterday. I mean, it was filed, it was fine, but it was one that kinda did all the right things, just not necessarily in the right order. Like Raheem Sterling going through on goal. I'm not happy with it, but, anyway, last night was as exciting for a Sunday newspaper beast as I had hoped it would be and I think the office are feeling it too. About 20 minutes after first edition came a jumbo email from the sports editor asking for as many suggestions as I can make for pieces in the event of England reaching the World Cup final. "24 pages ... put your thinking caps on ... ALL IDEAS considered!" We literally haven't had one conversation since the group stage in which he hasn't said, "It's coming home, my friend".

Sweden were possibly the second-least gifted side England have faced here (after Panama) but they were very difficult in their way. And that way involved playing old-fashioned, break-up-the-game, long balls/second balls, 4-4-f***ing-2. You had to glance at the team sheet just to double-check the manager wasn't called Nils Warnock or Mike Bassettsson. England had to trawl through their memory banks to recall how to play against this kind of stuff, and it took a while for them to remember that passing, movement, speed and getting between the lines were key.

Yet the game was comfortable for them in the end, or at least as comfortable as a World Cup quarter-final ever could be. Pickford had to make a couple of fine late saves but, even if one had gone in, I never thought Sweden had it in them to score twice.

It's funny being at the World Cup and yet missing out on a huge part of the World Cup experience, which is the reaction and communal match-watching back home. But from all the footage of loons shinning up lamp posts in Borough Market, the beach going mad at Brighton and Stormzy stopping his set at the Wireless Festival to do an acapella *It's Coming Home*, it appears that back home is having a good one.

Yet, it seems there is also still some negativity. "Calm down journos. England haven't played anyone of note," remains a Twitter theme. But tell me, who is "of note" in Russia? This is not a World Cup of outstanding sides, but one where you meet the diverse challenges set before you and take your opportunities. England have been doing that. This is a cup competition. You ride your draw, you adapt, you roll on.

Just because Sweden were a bit basic it doesn't mean, say, Belgium would have beaten them. They won Germany's group, put Italy out in the play-offs, got past Holland in qualifying and beat France in Stockholm. They're rugged, awkward. Similarly, who is to say Colombia aren't "of note"? They had one of the best centre-backs in the tournament, colossal willpower, some great individual skill and more street smarts than *The Wire* series 1-5. It strikes me that what England have done very well is handle completely different oppositions and styles – teams from four continents so far.

And apart from the 'B teams' match with Belgium they haven't been behind in any game. They've scored loads of goals (who cares if they're from set-pieces, set-pieces count too) and conceded just once in open play. They have a great spirit, a great outlook, the mindset of an ego-free team having an adventure together, enjoying themselves and not over-thinking. There is something in their attitude of Leicester in 2015-16. They're ignoring what others say, living in the moment, believing in themselves and are staying stress-free.

Pat Riley, "one of basketball's winningest coaches", as the Americans would say, wrote a book called *The Winner Within* in which he described the various stages of a successful team's evolution. England are taking those sweet footsteps he describes as The Innocent Climb. They are innocent about the trappings success might bring, or the pitfalls that might stop them getting there. Instead they're finding it great fun trying to ascend towards the prize. Good luck to them. This is great for all of us, even the Scots in the press pack.

After The Innocent Climb, there's a danger stage that Riley identifies as The Disease of Me. It's what might well have afflicted Germany at this tournament, but that is for another day.

— *Day 26, July 9*
This Team (2)

Nice pic, isn't it? My team. These are the Sunday newspaper soldiers covering England at the World Cup, minus a great friend, the *Sunday Mirror*'s Simon Mullock. Si has been with us at other times but flew off from Samara. Good lad, Si: over a Hoegaarden at Samara airport he was off on one of his two favourite subjects, Roddy Frame. The other is Manchester City. He is also a fantastic teller of old press box war stories.

The lads are all like that, they love their football and especially the business we're in, but all have other dimensions and depths. So in the photo you have, beside me, Rob Draper, *Mail on Sunday*, big brain, big thinker and very much his own man; a friend that you admire. He was only a second or two off Commonwealth Games standard when a young middle-distance athlete and he has dug out award- winning news stories about drugs and corruption in sport. Beside him, there's Steve Bates, *Sunday People*, whose effervescence has brightened many a mission we've been on; a Mr Man Utd and as streetwise a football reporter as they come. Warm, great company, superb at the job.

Behind him, there's Paul Hetherington, the kindest of colleagues, another teller-supreme of battlefield anecdotes, and someone who (like Steve) reminds me of my Scottish football reporting roots. The older guys I worked with then had proper contacts, proper relationships with managers and players, born from a slightly different era when press people and football people were closer to each other. Paul, however, has one great cross to bear. He's a Sunderland supporter.

Finally, to Paul's right, there's Mike McGrath, of *The Sun on Sunday*. 'Skybar' as he is sometimes called, and I've never asked why. You'd be hard pressed to meet someone more liked by the rest of the pack than Mike. He just has a way about him. Brilliant at relationships with contacts too, which is why he is soon to leave us, having been given a wider brief by his office. Mike's a decent footballer, too. For an Aussie, anyway.

So, that's the team I'm part of here. And this was us, yesterday afternoon, on a boat trip round St Petersburg. We've all been here approaching a month and have seen almost nothing of the city, because we've been working. I know that will be hard for many to believe. One of the most common questions you get as a Sunday guy is "Okay, so you go to a match on Saturday, but what do you do for the rest of the week?" The answer is straightforward: our expenses (that's not really the answer). I wanted to show you the 'Sundays' team to try to offer another little insight into our trade. It is one which has surprised a lot of my mates. The assumption from the outside, fuelled by portrayals of journalism on TV and in films, is that reporters from rival newspapers are enemies, locked in ruthless competition. The reality is that they tend to be friends. Indeed the biggest rivalries and enmities are often found among colleagues on the same paper.

Journalists from opposing titles become pals because they are sent out into the field together. The normal trip or story or match or press conference will involve one reporter per paper, deployed to cover it. There are hundreds of such 'missions' every season, so you spend an awful lot of time with your rivals – and far, far less with colleagues from your own title. Ergo, the 'rival' scribes are the ones who end up your mates.

There is another layer to it, which is that ours is a difficult job and sometimes the only way to accomplish things is to work together – trade phone numbers, exchange pieces of information, agree a co-ordinated approach in a group interview or press conference. Some groups of journalists even like to huddle together and agree the 'line' for the next day – a story that everyone is going to file. Safety/strength in numbers and all that. In my experience, this happens less in Sundays groups than groups of daily reporters – I think because our training is to be independent, but also that there is less pressure on us from editors to not 'miss' the story (so long as we have something distinctive of our own to file). This group approach, and the dynamic of rivals becoming pals is not unique to sports reporting – war correspondents and lobby journalists are just two groups who operate in very similar ways.

Anyway, I started today's entry with the intention of

writing about the England team, part 2, so here goes. I've seen more talented England sides. I've seen better World Cup semi-finalists. I've reported on players who were far bigger news. I've reported on England teams that might well beat the current one (I'm thinking 1996 and 1998).

But I haven't reported on an England team that is as much a team, nor one I've more admired. Indeed, this one might even exceed 1996's in being the best-coached. The players:

- Jordan Pickford: Still super-young in goalkeeping terms (he has 15+ years ahead of him if he lives right and has luck with injuries). Developing all the time. Fabulous mentality. One of the best keepers with his feet I've seen, up there with the best European and South American guys. His flat, driven, long passes out to his wing-backs are a thing of beauty. Remember: he arrived at this World Cup without having ever played a competitive international

- Kyle Walker: Was once averse to communicating publicly because of a few hits he took on the front and back pages earlier in his career, but is making up for it now. Perhaps the king of the England players on Twitter, always funny and apt there. Engaging personality and a superb interviewee. The quickest player in the team over 100m ('You know what forwards are like,' he grins, 'quick off the blocks but they fade'). Has blossomed tactically under Guardiola. Improving defender, excellent passer

- John Stones: To think I wondered whether he should start. One of England's players of the tournament, discovering an aggression and authority when attacking aerial balls we didn't know he had. The class of his first touch has never been in doubt, nor his composure with the ball at his feet, and the defensive errors he used to make by over-playing in the wrong situation barely resurface now

- Harry Maguire: Called 'Slab 'ead' by Jamie Vardy, which is nearly up there with the two best nicknames for defenders I've heard of: 'Bombscare' for Olivier Tebily (a description of his and others' terror whenever he received the ball). And 'Musselburgh' for Justin Edinburgh (think about it). Brave, imposing, becoming unstoppable in the air, but also England's best defender at bringing the ball out, including Stones

- Kieran Trippier: Has grown from high-class to world-class before our eyes in Russia. Probably the best deliverer of a set-piece England have had since Beckham (Gerrard's delivery was sensational, it's just that he quite often left dead balls to others). Has fantastic stamina and energy, and also consistency and steadiness. Almost the ideal modern wing-back

- Ashley Young: The old head, the streetwise competitor, the 'necessary nark' a team needs – someone to get in the opposition's heads and the ref's ear. Has transformed himself by moving further back but his wing-past makes him very useful when he gets in positions around the box. Defensively, he may sometimes still understandably get out of position, but one-v-one he's as good as England have. Handled Salah extraordinarily well when United played Liverpool

- Jordan Henderson: The second captain. Have such admiration for him as a player, because he is one who has been asked to fill several roles in his career and has always applied himself to each with incredible determination and football intelligence. Now a 'pivot', he has been better defensively than I'd have ever imagined when watching him as an attacking midfielder in his younger days. Great positioning. Keeps the ball circulating. Has hit some great passes at this tournament

- Jesse Lingard: A players' player and a connoisseur's player. Essential for the team. A real facilitator, forever on the move and either drawing opponents away to make spaces for others, or playing quick exchanges with team-mates to bring them into play. It still tickles me that his granddad is a champion weightlifter, given there is barely an ounce on Jesse

- Dele Alli: Great to see him score and then immediately, and visibly, swell in confidence against Sweden. Still so young. Such an athlete. What a great sense he has for timing a run on the blindsides of opponents to arrive in space in the box. Still a mystery why it took a PL club so long to sign him from MK Dons

- Raheem Sterling: Probably need to do a whole post on Sterling. Without his movement, without his ability to take defences both ways, either dropping short to receive the ball in tight positions or running behind them with his pace, England would be a much flatter, one-dimensional team. Takes rare football intelligence to make the movements he does. His 'receiving skills' (particularly an ability to take the ball under pressure and turn) are also rare. His issue, at the moment, is that he's not scoring and this relates to a tendency to over-think when he's in the box, leading to wrong decisions. But I really do think goals will come for him, for England. He's very young too, and a sweet kid. That so many really seem to dislike him makes me think that either there are a large number of people in Britain who don't know football … or something worse

- Harry Kane: Goals. Goals. He scores goals. That's almost enough said, only to add that apart from doing this most important of things, he's also skilled when he drops in as a No.10 with an ability to hold the ball up, turn and play people in. He did a lot of really unselfish work for the team v Sweden. It's not my line, but it's true of him: not 10/10 at any one thing, but 8/10 in every category of a striker's game. Will end up England's top all-time scorer

That's it, a summary of the first England side to reach a World Cup semi in 28 years. I expect them to go one step further than that and to be an XI that is remembered. And it's as an XI they should be remembered, because they're so very much a team.

Danger! Extrapolators At Work

Sorry hipsters, but this has been your nightmare World Cup. Set-pieces rule. Jorge Sampaoli became a joke. Where are the true *trequartistas*? And even oikish old England have learned how to play in the half-spaces ... with Jesse Lingard! There are no mysteries any more. It's enough to make you choke on your soya lattes and sourdough cruffins.

And the biggest horror: the South Americans are gone, departing early and in mostly ignominy, and we are left with a European World Cup. Worse than that, a Premier League World Cup, where the teams who remain draw heavily from English clubs for their personnel. England, Belgium, France, Croatia: 38% of the players left in the tournament played in the Premier League last year. Poor hipsters, what is there left for you to sniff about when it comes to English football?

Well, hold on. Today's entry is about the danger of extrapolating, of making grand judgments based on a small cluster of events, a hazard that can so often trip us up – all of us – who watch and especially who write about football. Maybe it's happening here because of the identities of the four semi-finalists. England's presence and our familiarity with the players in the French and Belgian squads is creating a temptation to think and write that we are seeing some kind of shift in power in the world game towards the Premier League and therefore England.

John Bull is back, John Bull is best.

Even when we look at Croatia, the squad still here with the fewest Premier League players, we see the likes of Modric, Kramaric and Corluka, and perceive them as having been 'made' at Premier League clubs. "This World Cup Shows The Premier League Is No.1 Again" you read. But, actually, is that just a load of John Bull?

Now it is true that, for the first World Cup in a long time, England and the English game no longer seems behind the curve. It is also undeniable that it's been a great tournament for the Premier League which, on top of doing well in terms of number of players still left in, is getting to live out that old Gore Vidal line: "It is not enough to succeed; others must fail." Beyond its own success the Premier League can look at its two main rivals, La Liga and the Bundesliga, having calamities because of Spain and Germany's failures, with no little *schadenfreude*.

But I think we should be wary of talking about power-shifts just yet. How many matches have been played in Russia? 60 so far. Nowhere near a big enough sample-size to be making blanket statements. I mean, if Belgium had gone out to Japan, or if England hadn't won their penalty shoot-out versus Colombia, there'd be a very different narrative about where the power lies.

We've all been there as journalists. I know I have. Back around 2009, 2010, there was a real taste at my paper for stats-based analysis pieces. They're something I enjoy doing and I was always enthusiastic when an idea for one was suggested to me. The editor liked them. I remember one season, round about late September, being asked to produce a big feature on why so many goals were being scored in the Premier League. The idea was to try to identify a change in the competition. The campaign had started with an unusually high number of goals. I spoke to coaches, managers, analysts and found it easy enough with the help of a few charts to posit the idea that a range of factors (declining goalkeeping, new ball, a tweak to the offside rule) was heralding a new era of open football and primacy of attacking teams. Goodness knows, I even convinced myself.

But when the article was produced, one of the readers' comments struck me. "Isn't it just that we've had a lot of goals in the first few weeks?" I got that nagging twinge at the back of the conscience that comes when you're told something you immediately know is true, but aren't yet ready to accept. And the reader was right. It had just been a freak few weeks and the scoring levels settled down across the whole season. I still do those analysis pieces from time to time but am much more cautious now.

We live in a world where extrapolation is king. There is a desperation to find meaning so we go overboard about small events. Increasingly, we live our lives online, where what we do is tracked and algorithms try to predict what we are going to want to do or be interested in next. You look at one Airbnb in Barcelona for ten seconds and suddenly you're bombarded by pop-up ads for hotels and apartments near Las Ramblas. What's really happening, at this World Cup, with all the 'Premier League is king again' stuff is three things ... I think.

- First, as I've said, there's the freak element. Japan don't throw away a 2-0 lead v Belgium, Colombia win on pens v England, Russia do the same to Croatia and there'd be no pattern to look at. There'd be four teams left whose players are spread fairly evenly across various leagues.
- Second, we're looking at it through our British lens. The French could extrapolate differently. They could observe the success of their own team and then the

fact several of Belgium's best players, notably Eden Hazard, were developed in French football and say that this World Cup proves the enduring strength of the French academies. They could add in the success of Neymar and Cavani and say the top of their game, ie Paris Saint Germain, is in great health too. Or Africans could point out that exactly half (23 out of 46) of the players in the squads for the France v Belgium semi-final are of African descent, and argue it has been a tournament that shows the great potential of their own continent's teams – if only the game's economics were different and their FAs could get things right. It's that old thing of seeing what you want to see.

• Thirdly and this is where I think the truth lies, if it lies anywhere, what has really changed is the standard of coaching in the Premier League. Recent years have seen English clubs take a logical next step after many seasons of splurging on the most expensive players they could find. Clubs have also started splurging on the most expensive coaches. Guardiola is here. Klopp is here. Pochettino is here. Conte is here but Sarri may be coming. Mourinho remains. Ranieri did his thing at Leicester. In different ways, these top technicians have influenced Premier League players, causing England to do better and hasten the development of the young Belgians and Frenchmen who come to British shores (as young players from those countries historically do). Belgium owe Guardiola for De Bruyne, France can thank Ranieri and Conte for the rise of Kante. And of course the English players have been moulded by the coaches mentioned. Pochettino has almost been England's academy director in recent years. Klopp has had enormous influence on Henderson. Thank Mourinho for Ashley Young's reinvention as a full-back/wing-back and believing in Lingard. Guardiola, of course, has been of enormous importance to Sterling and Stones. Gary Neville spoke very well about this in today's *Times*. "There's no doubt there's an influence from the coaches in the Premier League, Guardiola in particular, the playing out from the back, the influence on John Stones, but that's exactly what there should be, a transfer of knowledge. It's about time English football took advantage of that," he said. The mini development 'boom' in the Premier League is not all foreign work – full acknowledgement must be given to Sean Dyche and his phenomenal record of producing England players at Burnley – but Neville's point rings true.

So, in conclusion, I don't know if this World Cup shows The Premier League Is Back or that John Bull is better than Juan Torro or that there has been any power-shift at all. I just know to be careful about jumping to big conclusions.

For example, take my breakfast plate in St Petersburg today. Does it mean that I *always* like to start the day with an odd combo of cheese and fish? Or that I was late to breakfast and grabbed a hotchpotch of what was left? Friends with experience of my timekeeping might know the real answer.

Prediction today: France 0 Belgium 0 (France on penalties)

Player to watch: N'Golo Kante. At the time of the 2010 World Cup he was 19, on an amateur contract, and getting to training at his new club Boulogne on a child's scooter. At the time of the 2014 tournament he was 23 and still hadn't played in Ligue 1. I love his story, and watching his almost peerless tactical diligence and football intelligence

What happened next: Belgium had the ball but France made the chances, and after Raphael Varane's goal in the quarters, his centre-back partner Samuel Umtiti was the hero. Kante, as ever, set the table with his mastery of space and telepathic anticipation of opponents' passes as his reputation rose yet further in Russia

— Day 28, July 11
SMC (Stadium Media Centre)

Good evening from St Petersburg, with 40 minutes to go before France v Belgium. In this first tournament in memory where things exceed, rather than fall short of, expectations, I'm looking forward to a bit of an epic here. The two best teams in the competition probably, and each with different weak spots and strengths. I'm writing this now, rather than tomorrow, to try to get ahead of the game. If England get to the World Cup final, Thursday-Saturday will probably be the busiest 72 hours of my newspaper career. I want to clear the decks and this entry will have to be short.

But, the Stadium Media Centre: I've wanted to tell you about these since this blog began. They are an integral element of any tournament experience. And not in a good way. Imagine a brightly lit, over air-conditioned hangar filled with formica desks and plastic chairs. Rows upon rows. Plugs and cheap lamps. Contradictory signage and young, overly-happy volunteers who do their best to help but don't really have the linguistic skills or information base to really be of use. Now imagine this pitiless space filled with journalists: writers, photographers, radio people, TV crews and that odd bloke from Eastern Europe who looks so much like Borat that surely he must be a hoaxer (mind you, if so, he has been keeping it up for the last four World Cups).

What we're talking about is journalism's version of a battery farm. Take us to some beautiful city, in some exotic country, at some exciting tournament but then force us inside this nasty space and drain our resistance and independence away, until what you're left with are poor, enervated creatures, ready for the slaughter. That appears to be FIFA's idea anyway. "Brighter lights!" you can imagine Gianni Infantino yelling. "Cheaper chairs!

"We will break them!

"They *will* write something good about VAR and the FIFA Forward Programme."

To ramp up the feeling of oppression, FIFA has a new wheeze at these finals. Weedy guys with lanyards, sour faces and little monitoring machines prowl the SMCs, like Infantino's traffic wardens, looking to detect and root out personal hotspot devices. They admonish you if you're found using one and maybe it will be confiscated. The idea is that everyone has to use FIFA's WiFi.

Why? Who knows. Originally we imagined it was part of a deal with Putin to aid Russian cyber-hacking. Our offices told us on no account to use WiFi here, but in the SMCs there's no choice. But apparently this has been going on at other FIFA tournaments of late. So it is maybe just another effort at stamping out journalists' individualism. Perhaps there is even some unseen commercial motive that will become clear, who knows? It's just one more thing. For two World Cups now, for example, you can only buy food in the SMC canteens by cash or using VISA. No Mastercard. VISA being a FIFA sponsor.

Whether you'd want to buy food in an SMC is another matter. The stuff they serve? Another thing that reminds you of battery farming: it is slop, slurry, the sort of thing animal rights protesters would picket over if it was served to battery chickens. The turkey sauce option for accompaniment to the rubber SMC pasta is indescribable, both in its colourless colour and its slimy consistency. Rob Draper had a bit of salmon in one SMC and felt like vomiting for days. I think I've already told you about the so-called fish burgers. The only sensible options here are cake (very good), salad (can't really go wrong), and pasta with just pesto: you can get used to rubber, as long as it's flavoured. Don't think that SMC slop is just a Russia thing, or even a FIFA thing. The food in Brazil was brutal but not as bad as at Euro 2012 in Ukraine. In Kharkiv one of the options was a whole boiled egg, the yolk greeny, served in a plastic box in which it floated in water. SMC food is so bad that even at Euro 2016, in gourmet France, it was unremittingly, unpalatably awful.

I've always believed that the organisations and institutions we deal with demonstrate their true feelings towards the media via food. At Manchester City, for five or six seasons following the Abu Dhabi takeover, they wanted to charm us, so the food at the Etihad was the best in the country. It's still good, but you can see the quality and budget put towards it gradually dropping off, the more successful City become and less they feel they need us.

Arsenal are consistently classy and thoughtful, even offering tubs of ice-cream to take out with a coffee to your seat, but is this because, without success on the pitch, they need to keep us sweet. Chelsea is opulent: salmon, fine cheeses, artisan breads, a range of sweets and salads, and hot options. Their statement is: we're richest, we're best. Manchester United's offering is utterly disdainful: cake, sandwiches and cold chips, like a bad cricket tea. Vomit on that, suckers! It's very eloquent.

But no offering, not even UEFA's, is as contemptuous as turkey slime and fish burger slop. In the SMCs they break our spirit and then show that, deep down, beyond the chatty press releases, the stats packs, the forums and Infantino's cheesy smile, what is really going on is that they hate us.

Prediction today: England 2 Croatia 1

Player to watch: Raheem Sterling. Nearly every journalist watching England in Russia will tell you how fundamental Sterling is to England's strategy, and that he is performing well, except when he gets scoring chances. Admittedly, as a second-striker or No.10, he needs to score, and that is a not an inconsiderable glitch. But, overall, he has been good. Mr Hated One, silence the haters. Come on Raheem

What happened next: England started brilliantly and faded but the killer blow, from Mario Mandzukic in extra time, was far from inevitable. Sterling ended the tournament without a goal but had been a crucial element of the attack – at full tilt, a terrifying prospect for defenders

End of the World

In my first full-time job, as a trainee general reporter on the *Glasgow Herald*, I learned about one of the great newspaper concepts: The Freezer. The Obituaries pages? Well, they aren't written in the heat of the moment. Rather, 'obits' are crafted in the cold light of day, while the subject is still alive, and there is time to think through how to best sum up that person's life. Famous people won't know when, but once they get to a certain age, newspapers across the world will begin collating material for the event of their deaths. Maybe you turn 60, win a BAFTA, and some editor somewhere will tell some reporter 'we need an obit for them. Get it done and put it in The Freezer'.

The Freezer is a 'basket' (digital folder) accessible to the editors and sub-editors, to where obit pieces are filed. They are stored there, ready to be taken out and stuck on a page the moment a subject dies. Of course some live on and on, so their obits are regularly pulled from storage and amended/updated. The Queen Mother's obit was probably in and out of The Freezer more often than an ice cube tray in summer.

I've often thought there should be a special sports desk freezer for a particular article we all have to write at every tournament. The England Obit. It's that bit of writing we do every two years when England have just been dumped from finals, the nation is mourning, the players are dishevelled and the manager has lost his sheen. Since I've covered England the elements in such articles are pretty standard.

- Some key player has malfunctioned under pressure
- The manager's limitations have been shown up
- How come these foreign chaps pass the ball so well?
- How come England don't?
- Why is there nothing coming through?
- We need a player like (Pirlo/Suarez/Figo/insert name of star from oppo which have just humbled the Three Lions)
- If our players trained more and spent less on their watches…
- The rugby/cycling team have the right idea
- There should be a review/think tank/something
- We should follow the Spanish/German/Icelandic (okay maybe not the Icelandic) model

The obits from tournament to tournament end up being so similar that I've wondered whether we should just pre-write them, drop them in a sports desk freezer and publish right on the whistle in England's exit game. Why not? We live in a world of instant analysis, of our online eds asking for 'Five things we learned from United v City', "to be filed at half-time please".

But I'm on the train back to St Petersburg from Moscow after England's 2-1 defeat by Croatia and this feels different. I mean, we could go down the whole 'foreigners were better, Premier League is overrated, where is England's Modric', route, and that would make for punchy copy. But it would also be disingenuous. England changed. For the first tournament since Euro 2004, they leave in a better position than they started, with the feeling things are moving forward. And yet, at the same time, familiar faults resurfaced at Luzhniki Stadium last night, so our obits will need to be nuanced. What I saw in the game and how it relates to England 'progress' or otherwise: Elements of performance that were hugely classy from the three England players with claims to be in 'team of the tournament' contention and believe me, having even one England player in 'team of tournament' contention would be progress. These players are Pickford, Stones and Trippier. Pickford's distribution was again exceptional. He has uncanny ability, under pressure, to switch the ball between his feet and get away a kick that is not a clearance, but a pin-point 50-yard pass. Stones again demonstrated leadership, judgment in when to leave his defensive line to engage opponents, set-piece goal threat and calmness on the ball. Trippier's running, delivery and competitiveness were all to be marvelled at once more. Yet Stones' one momentary lapse in concentration led to Croatia's goal, while Perisic – Trippier's direct opponent – was man of the match. And Pickford's long kicking contributed to England going too direct as the game got away from them. So what to make of that all?

Raheem Sterling was once again indispensable in attack, the only England man continually opening the opposition up, with his elusiveness, speed, and dangerousness on the ball. Yet he's a No.10 who failed to score, had just one shot on target and completed only 91 passes in five games at these finals. What to make of him?

Harry Kane was jaded, missed twice from close range when his one big opening came, making the wrong decision too (should have passed instead of trying to score from a tight angle and hitting the post). He scored only once – a penalty – in the knockout stage. But Kane put in a selfless shift in other ways, dropping into midfield to try to help control Luka Modric, and to leave space for Sterling to run into. He will win the Golden Boot. He has a new legion of admirers around the world, who have seen close-up what we see in the Premier League every week. So there are complexities there, too.

Gareth Southgate? Nuances again. In so many ways, England's star of the tournament. However, the momentum of that match swung against England and stayed in Croatia's favour for a good 60, 70 minutes, and there was nothing that he changed. Okay, his bench wasn't replete with options, but it is a coach's job to do something.

I could go on.

What I'm trying to show, I guess, is that it is a complicated England inquest this time. An obit which needs to be finely judged. I have to get working on one for Sunday and I need to gather my thoughts. I'm going to try to watch the whole game back in the quiet of my hotel room, and hope to speak to Southgate at some point before writing. It's probably going to be a 'on the one hand, yet on the other hand' article. A bit of classic broadsheet fence-sitting. Hey, I've had 23 years of that and don't mind the splinters. The quick summary, right now, would be ... England: young team, young manager, both of whom have been revelations yet have scope to improve. Those damn foreigners: still better at passing the ball.

Anyway, onto the biggest Three Lions World Cup question of all, one which popped into my mind last night in Moscow, one which arises at every England game: why, oh why, when it's one of the easiest tunes in the world; why, even with someone leading the singing and words on the big screen ... why can't those English supporters sing their own national anthem? By the end of "send her victorious" they've raced ahead so much they're on "long to reign over us." Every time.

Root and branch review of the fans, I say.

— Day 30, July 13
Beating the Bridges

It was when our barman raised his glass and said "Davai!" that I knew I wasn't going to beat the bridges. "Davai!" is one of about ten words the Russians have for cheers!, and it's no surprise that their drinking vocab is as extensive as that of Eskimos with snow. They're world class at it; if drinking was the Davis Cup, it would be them in the world group alongside the Irish and us Scots.

"Davai!"

Back in St Petersburg we had a wee night out, realising it was our last chance of the trip. Today there's a mountain of writing to do: those England obits and tomorrow there's the third-placed game. Plus further travelling. On Sunday a lot of reporters are going home, while the rest of us head to Moscow again for the final. After the tournament, Mike McGrath is being reassigned to a daily newspaper beat, so last night was something of a send-off for him, his farewell from the Sunday pack. We were out in Rubinshteyna: now that place, as a street of bars and restaurants, is also something world class.

We ended up in a secret drinking hole, the back bar of a restaurant. They lead you through the kitchens to get there. Rob Draper has been going to this restaurant, on and off, for a month without knowing the bar was there. It's secret. You have to get the nod and be escorted in.

Of course journalists love finding secrets, so we adored it, and it was tiny, it was atmospheric, it had French hip hop playing, and it had Lagavulin. And when the barman lined them up and accepted the offer of a drink for himself, grinning "davai!" as he raised a Monkey Shoulder, that's

138   Deadlines and Darts with Dele

when I knew the bridges were going to beat me.

The bridges? Forgive me if I've already written about this – this is day 30, there's still Lagavulin in the system, and I simply can't remember – but St Petersburg is built on a series of islands, ten of them, connected by numerous bridges. At around 1.30am the bridges go up to allow ships to sail in, and they stay raised until nearly 5am.

Rubinshteyna is in the Tsentralny district and my hotel is on Vasilyevsky island, so to get home I really needed to be in a taxi and across the water by 1.30. Later, and the bridges would be up and that's what happened. It's still possible to get back to Vasilyevsky in such circumstances, but it means your taxi driving all the way out of town, looping round on a ring road, crossing the big sea bridge (which never goes up) and going across far off Kretovsky Island before heading back into the city from the other side.

That's what I, in my Yandex, ended up doing and it was fine and you can never regret Lagavulin(s). But that St Petersburg moment, which locals face nightly – do I beat the bridges? – is an illustration of how certain things in life come down to a now-or-never moment.

Reading this morning's papers, everyone is (rightly) still very positive about England, but one piece stood out: Jamie Carragher's *Telegraph* column. Jamie's tone was slightly different. "One of football's great myths is the idea that the agony of defeat will be the catalyst for future success," he wrote. His point is that, as great a ride as England had, it doesn't necessarily follow that the next tournament will be better, no matter that England are young, will learn from their experience, and will probably go to Euro 2020 with an improved squad, with wonderkids like Jadon Sancho, Phil Foden and Ryan Sessegnon joining the group.

Jamie's reasoning is that sport is often as much about

opportunity as it is about talent. And reading him today took me back to a conversation we had in 2013-14, a few weeks before the end of a season where Liverpool were surprising everyone with a thrilling title bid. I was interviewing Jamie for the paper and we were sitting in a box at Anfield, with him preparing to do some filming for Sky. Looking out on the stadium, as fans filed in for an evening game, all I could see was hope.

I could see a young manager on the up (Brendan Rodgers), a team with great young talents (in Raheem Sterling, Daniel Sturridge, Jordan Henderson and Jon Flanagan), a superstar-on-the-rise in Luis Suarez. "Even if Liverpool don't win this title race, they've really taken steps forward this season and will be able to make an even better bid next season," I said. Jamie shook his head. "Nah, doesn't work like that," he said.

This was the pro talking. There are no guarantees in football, Jamie explained, you don't know what's going to happen. All you know is what's in front of you, and in front of Liverpool was a golden opportunity that might not come again. That perspective stuck with me and of course, over the ensuing 12-18 months, Carra was proved right. Rodgers' regime went into reverse, Suarez wanted to go, Sterling too. Sturridge got injured. Rivals got better. Mario Balotelli arrived.

There are plenty other examples in sport of teams or individuals passing up a golden chance and then never getting a better one. Colin Montgomerie messing up when leading the 1994 US Open and then spending the next 20 years missing out on majors. Paula Radcliffe going into the Athens Olympics marathon as overwhelming favourite but having a meltdown before the eyes of the world. She quit and sat down, sobbing, by the side of the road. She was never the same. Did England fail to beat the bridges in Russia 2018? They had their chance and didn't take it. Croatia were a better side but England were 22 minutes from a World Cup final on Wednesday in Moscow. After their semi-final in 1990, England didn't even qualify for the 1994 World Cup. They won't get as good a draw at the next tournament and if England are young, well, France are younger. Kylian Mbappe ain't going anywhere.

There's an odd feeling among the press pack. "Result of the tournament – got my flights home confirmed," said one of the lads last night and we were all a bit demob happy, relieved that the tsunami of work that would have come had England beaten the Croats was no longer heading our way. But deep down I think everyone had a more powerful feeling, and that was regret. We'd have worked round the clock, survived the deadlines, written our pieces and got through until Sunday. And then we'd have been watching the team we cover in a World Cup final, an experience we would have never forgotten.

Actually, when you don't beat the bridges in St Petersburg you do get another chance to reach your destination, you just have to take the longer way there. Maybe that will be how it is for England and they'll be champions in one of the next tournaments to come. But maybe not.

Gettin' Jiggy Wit It

Something great happened in the SMC (a first!) yesterday. Will Smith, purveyor of The Official Song for FIFA World Cup 2018 (that's trademarked, baby), was giving a press conference in Moscow and it was playing on the screens of the St Petersburg Stadium media centre. The sound was off, but you could see Smith grinning his genial grin and effortlessly managing to look honoured to simply be part of football's big global party and not at all contractually obliged.

Simultaneously, in the press conference tent, Fabian Delph was taking questions about the third-placed game. They piped his audio in through the SMC speakers. So, you had Smith on the screens, talking, but Delph's audio. "Ah thought we wuh realleh realleh gorn to do it ugunst Croashuh," came Delph's broad Leeds accent as Smith's lips moved almost in perfect sync. The fresh prince of good clean family rap has never sounded quite like that.

Outside, through the windows, the sun was sparkling on the waters of the Gulf of Finland and cruise ships were coming in. A relaxed vibe because, well, who cares about the third-placed game? Delph gettin' jiggy with it was one more moment to smile about in the most fun of World Cups.

I'm writing this just as England v Belgium is about to start, having just got through all my *Sunday Times* stuff – the England obit, a last David Moyes column and an 'editor's wish' piece, inspired by his wife, for almost the first time, quite enjoying the football. Over the last four weeks England, and in particular Nice Gareth, have drawn so many people in. How, this article was commissioned to discuss, do the Football Association keep ordinary people – especially editors' wives – engaged with the England team?

Okay, half-time now, Belgium 1-0 up, playing the better football, and England a little casual. Raheem Sterling and Danny Rose are off, Marcus Rashford and Jesse Lingard are on, whereas the Belgians – rather inconsiderately – are keeping Eden Hazard, Kevin De Bruyne, Vincent Kompany, Alex Witsel and Youri Tielemans on the pitch. There have been Mexican waves, there have been klaxons, there has been rather too much heard from the England band. It's all a bit too much like a Wembley friendly. You'd almost rather listen to a FIFA song.

I thought I'd do my team of the tournament today and here goes. Things I noticed when picking this: a plethora of goalkeeping and centre-back candidates but no convincing candidate for left-back.

4-3-3

- Danijel Subasic (Croatia) – Pickford, Lloris, Courtois and Cho Hyun-Woo (who had that astonishing performance v Germany) came close, but Subasic has been extraordinary. Penalty shoot-out heroics, great authority throughout and a jaw-dropping save from Kane in the semi-final

- Kieran Trippier (England) – Had a strange semi-final, curling in a superb free-kick and defending feistily at times. But all while being outplayed by the man of the match, Perisic. Glad I wasn't doing the match ratings, don't know what I'd have given him. But for the rest of the tournament

Trippier's contributions were unquestionable. Assists galore thanks to providing the best England set-piece delivery since Gerrard and Beckham

- Yerry Mina (Colombia) – Have never seen such leadership and such influence upon a team from a young centre-half. The towering, powerful, fearless Mina marshalled Colombia with a mix of muscle and intelligence, and scored three great headers from set-pieces. Didn't deserve to go out of the competition so early and I'm convinced we're seeing the early stages of the career of a truly great defender

- Raphael Varane (France) – Exudes class, oozes calm, still young but an utter thoroughbred. Has already won about a hundred Champions Leagues with Real Madrid and may well become a world champion tomorrow. Umtiti, his partner, was considered too; also Vida, Stones and Maguire. But Mina and Varane just had that extra authority

- Lucas Hernandez (France) – Found this the hardest position to fill. Marcelo (I'm a big fan of the little madman) got injured and, while Rodriguez of Switzerland was decent, he didn't do enough. Considered selecting Vertonghen and moving him out to the left but that's cheating. So I've gone for Hernandez, who has been pretty solid (as you'd expect from any Atletico Madrid defender) and has put some good crosses in

- Luka Modric (Croatia) – I watched back the England v Croatia game and saw a recurring image in the second half: England players running like crazy (usually back towards their own goal) and wee Modric just standing still, loitering in space, waiting where he knew he could receive the ball, simply letting the game come to him. His receiving skills under pressure, his passing and game management put him right up among the world's very top players

- N'Golo Kante (France) – For a long time all people talked about was how much ground Kante covered. Actually his game is a lot more focused than that. His real asset is intelligence. His positioning is magnificent and the timing of his interceptions and tackles incredible. He has been the fulcrum that has allowed the French team to play and be much better than at Euro 2016

- Antoine Griezmann (France) – I'm cheating a bit here because Griezmann's more a second striker than No.10, but I figure that, with Kante and Modric running the game, you could play any formation in front of them. Such an ingenious and economical player. Started the tournament a little slowly but has got better and better towards the business end

- Eden Hazard (Belgium) – His performance in Belgium's semi-final v France was one of the best displays in defeat I've ever seen. So sharp, so brave in always taking the ball, telling with nearly every intervention: true captain stuff. He twice completed ten dribbles in a match, breaking World Cup dribble records that have stood since 1966

- Kylian Mbappe (France) – At what was possibly Ronaldo and Messi's last World Cup, it was appropriate that a new superstar stepped forward. And kind of great that it wasn't the diving, self-centred Neymar. Mbappe has been electric and the best teenager to grace this stage since Pele. When he puts on the afterburners and scorches past a defender it's one of the great sights in football

- Ivan Perisic (Croatia) – Against England, Perisic reminded me of one of the pros who sometimes play against us journo chumps in a media game. Just more savvy, more crafty, more skilled and more a winner than anyone else on the pitch. Mourinho was mocked for wanting to sign him for £50m a year ago – but now we see why. Would be very successful in the Premier League

Prediction today: Belgium 3 England 1; I'm cheating by posting this after the match, but this is what I bet on in the journalists' sweep before kick off. Expected England to at least score, and Eric Dier had a magnificent effort. Kane was appalling though

Player to watch: Serena Williams. Look, this is a third-placed play-off bobbins ... what are you doing with the football on? Turn over and watch the tennis

What happened next: A game that merits its place in the dubious canon of third-place play-offs. Belgium benefited from technical superiority and greater depth of top-grade talent. Serena went down in straight sets to Angelique Kerber

The Final JamJar

When I was younger, and I can't remember whether it was my brother, a pal, or even a gremlin in my head, someone changed the lyrics to *Final Countdown* by Europe and sang "it's the final jamjar", in Joey Tempest's slightly high-pitched, accented voice. Since then, I've never been able to hear anything else when the song is played. It's *The Final Jamjar* to me.

This is not a frivolous intro. Well, not entirely. Because substitute "jamjar" for "countdown" and all the attempted drama in the song drains away and I'm going to a World Cup final today and don't we always fear that big football finals are going to be let downs? That they won't follow their scripts? That the words will change and drama will drain away?

This fear is especially vivid, I think, when it is a game like today's. France v Croatia, a game involving two teams about whom we're essentially neutral. We set aside an evening or a pub afternoon for a group of footballers we're not actually that connected with, so will they still engage us?

"Finals seldom live up to their billing," is the cliche. But you know what? I think there's a collective brain fade here. I think there's an odd reverse of how human psychology normally works. Normally, as a resilient species, we suppress hurt or difficult experience and persuade ourselves to go again – that's what makes women have another go at childbirth. But the opposite seems to happen with finals. The Fear of the Big Match Letdown is such that we suppress *positive* experiences and worry too much about being disappointed. Because I've been going back over all the finals I have ever attended ... and, my goodness, the list is absolutely crammed with good games.

In fact, it makes me think that the big cup final is the least likely type of game to be a squib. Here goes. Today will be my fourth World Cup final, I've been to two European Championship finals, I've been to 16 Champions League finals. My memory gets a bit sketchy with FA Cup finals because I used to come down from Glasgow and cover them even before I started with the English *Sunday Times*. But not every year. So, totting it up, I think I've been to 19 FA Cup finals. The League Cup final? Now, bear in mind two things:

a) They take place on Sundays, and Sunday journalists are like devout Presbyterians on the Isle of Lewis. Doesn't matter what you invite us to. Sunday is a day of rest.

b) When I started at the ST I learned a lot from the great Joe Lovejoy. Joe had a very firm view: "the knob-end cup final" he used to call it.

So, I've only been to two League Cup finals. Scottish Cups and Scottish League Cups? Between those attended as a journalist and those as a fan: 17. Add it all together and today's showpiece is the 60th final where I'll have been present in the stadium. And when I actually go through the previous 59, there have been so many more classics and thrillers than rubbish games.

Champions League finals are the most consistent, I think. My first was 2002, the ball dropping from an inky sky above old Hampden Park and Zidane nailing his beautiful volley. Then Milan 0 Juventus 0 (penalties). That was crap. But the next one was Istanbul. Then Paris, Henrik Larsson turning it Barcelona's way versus Arsenal with one of the great cameos.

Afterwards, Athens, an AC Milan masterclass. Then

Moscow, the Luzhniki where I'll be today and Manchester United 1 Chelsea 1 was one of the best matches I've seen in my entire life, because you had two utterly top-class teams utterly on top of their games. Until John Terry slipped, I don't remember a mistake in the whole 120+ minutes.

2009 and 2011, the wonder of Barcelona. 2012, Chelsea shocking Bayern. Throw in Bayern at Wembley, Barca in Berlin and then the takeover of the fixture by Real Madrid's slightly horrible but absolutely majestic current team.

FA Cup finals are generally fine, expansive matches played in Wembley sunshine. The Scottish finals of my youth were pretty good. So when I put it all down on paper I struggle to come up with a species of football match that has given me more consistent thrill and entertainment than finals.

Contrast them with derby matches. Now you're talking let-downs. So many derby matches are either too hectic or too cautious to be watchable. Sky Super Sundays? Anticlimaxes, a lot of them. League deciders or games on the last day of the season when the title is on the line? Now they tend to be good. But I'd contend that's because they are essentially cup finals in dynamic.

I haven't mentioned World Cup and Euros finals ... well, maybe this is where the fear comes from. They have been the least attractive games amid the various finals I've experienced. The three World Cup finals I've attended ended up going to extra-time after an attritional 90 minutes and produced a combined four goals in six hours of football. And of the two Euros finals I've been to, one was Portugal 0 Greece 1 in 2004. Now that really *was* a knob-end of a game.

Looking at other patterns is interesting. I jotted down, beside the actual victors' names, the team in that final that

I'd tipped to win. There were some games which appeared 50-50 beforehand (like that 2008 meeting between Chelsea and United) so I ignored those. So here's the thing. Out of my 59 previous finals, only four were won by the underdog side. Isn't that incredible ? Those four were ...

- Istanbul
- Chelsea beating Bayern in 2012
- Wigan upsetting Manchester City in the 2013 FA Cup final
- Birmingham winning the League Cup in 2011

So, out of 59 finals just four won by the unexpected team. I still can't get over this when I look at it. Especially because so many of the finals were tight, well-matched, knife-edge affairs, where the winning side had to really dig to prevail. For instance Germany in the last World Cup final really had to work to put away that inferior, dysfunctional (albeit still Messi-infused) Argentina team.

Likewise, in 2010, it was only a narrow win for imperious, 'peak' Spain versus Bert Van Marwijk's Dutch henchmen. In the Champions League, there were Real's very hard-fought victories over Atletico Madrid. So what does all this tell us? That finals are quite often gruelling, finely-poised wrestles ... where the best team then wins.

I also jotted down how finals were won, or what the factors were in those matches. Conclusions: Champions League finals tend to come down to great collective play, victory achieved by the side that executes brilliant team patterns (a Barcelona, a Milan, a Bayern) or where a combination of their great individuals step up at once (the Real Madrid template).

The exceptions: Istanbul and Chelsea in Munich stemmed

from single players having the games of their lives and using their exceptional willpower to bend the whole darn shooting match their way. Steven Gerrard for Liverpool, Didier Drogba for Chelsea. This is kind of logical. We see in other sport examples of powerful individualism where very occasionally one person is just so unbelievably good that all other competitors, even competitors of the highest level, are forced to bow to them.

Maybe, the one absolute outlier, for which there was no rational explanation, was Birmingham beating Arsenal. Wait ... *there's* the explanation. Arsenal.

My three World Cup finals had spookily similar dynamics. Here are the reasons I wrote down for why Germany beat Argentina four years ago:

- Collective prowess
- Willpower
- Small moments
- Confidence (based on their journey as a side and previous successes) that they'd prevail when it came to the crunch
- Good substitutions
- An extra-time goal scored by an attacking midfielder playing in the left channel

Exactly the same was true of Spain's triumph in 2010. Both games also featured certain odd refereeing decisions. And they were introduced by Latino Official FIFA World Cup (trademarked, baby) songs, from Shakira and Pitbull.

On that (musical) note I came out of the mixed zone in St Petersburg last night to find the England Team bus waiting to leave the stadium. Utter tunes were blaring from it. First, *Get Down On It* and then Kurtis Blow. I've been a little harsh about their football shortcomings in today's *Sunday Times* but I've got to hand it to Southgate and his lads: there has never been a more likeable, more good-taste England team.

Right, about to leave a shopping mall in Moscow for Game 64. The last of this World Cup. The final jamjar. I fear it might not be much of a spectacle, but history suggests that fear is misplaced.

Prediction today (one last chance to get one of these right): France 2 Croatia 0

Player to watch: Dejan Lovren. I've done Kylian Mbappe and spoken about Antoine Griezmann, Raphael Varane, N'Golo Kante, Luka Modric, Ivan Perisic, Danijel Subasic in my team of the tournament. So a mention for big Dejan. One of the loveliest, heart-on-sleeve sportsmen you'll meet; a guy I had a memorable lunch with in Aigburth two months ago. Capable of an outstanding performance or a glaring mistake. Which will it be today? He's always worth watching anyway, and on a personal level, I feel he's underrated and would like him to do well

What happened next: No big-game let-down here. Controversy, VAR, goals, big personalities and big errors. France claimed the crown and their young prince, Kylian Mbappe, scored the last of their four in the final. A fitting denouement to one of the great tournaments

— *Day 33, July 16*
Do Svidaniya

My World Cup ended in the lobby bar of the Radisson Slavyanskaya, at 3.30am, nursing one last Lagavulin (you've got to reward yourself) and listening to Carlos Queiroz tell his Fergie stories and talk about Persian hegemony in Iranian society. There was a table to our left where a Frenchwoman, clutching a plastic World Cup trophy, was having drinks with a guy wearing the Scotland away top plus kilt.

I was with Michael Church, an old pal from past World Cups: we first met in a SMC as young journalists at France 98. Michael is Northern Irish, specialises in Asia and lives in Hong Kong. We see each other every four years, each time a little older and balder. I'd been in Carlos's press conferences but had never spoken properly to him before last night: a fascinating man.

He has taken two countries to World Cups, managed Real Madrid and coached in Japan, Africa, UAE and New York. He is of underrated importance in Manchester United's history, instrumental to evolving United into the modern, adaptable, European side which reached three Champions League finals in four years from 2008-11 and featured Cristiano Ronaldo, Wayne Rooney, Carlos Tevez, Nemanja Vidic, Patrice Evra, Rio Ferdinand and Paul Scholes.

He loved Scholes. England weren't that far away at this World Cup, Carlos felt; they just needed one different type, an orchestrator who could put their foot on the ball in midfield. "This team ... with Scholes," he smiled. "Who knows?" I'd envisaged getting an early night so as to be fresh for travelling home today, but the best laid plans and all that. Anyway, a hotel lobby bar, a polyglot coaching legend, an old SMC pal (me and Mike worked out we've now done six tournaments together), nearby a random Scot with a plastic trophy ... that seemed a fitting *melange* with which to end another World Cup.

A World Cup I was pretty much dreading, but which has turned out to be the best one of my life. Now, from a chaotic Moscow Sheremetyevo airport, from an Uzbek restaurant, with a beer and a Margilan flat bread, I'm preparing to sign off from this blog. But before I go, here are some last reflections...

England

I've just been on Rodney Marsh's US internet radio show. Rodney said they are renaming an Underground station after Gareth Southgate and someone also claimed the good people of Crawley are planning a statue in Gareth's honour. Yet an agent told me that in victorious France the opinion was England were just a little bit *merde*, and that Harry Kane is being called the worst ever Golden Boot winner (how quickly people forget Oleg Salenko). Football is all about opinions, as they say.

Mine? That Southgate does deserve praise. Not a statue or a station, but certainly a solid pat on the back. He produced a unified and likeable England team, who played with pride and togetherness and (slightly) overachieved. He won a penalty shoot-out. He won an opening game. He didn't drink a pint of wine. He spoke with more intelligence, perspective and charisma than any current British politician is capable of. In terms of what has gone before with England, none of this is to be underestimated. Reporting on England at past tournaments has been like having a ringside seat as a clown car sputters into the centre of a ring and then lamely falls apart.

However, I feel the improvements Southgate brought largely involved those things around the edges. Culture. Psychology. Set-pieces. Practising penalties. Media. A good camp. He also came up with a system and formation that allowed him to get his best available players into the starting XI, and which gave England a level of ball retention, defensive solidity and pitch coverage that was sorely lacking in the tournaments of flat 4-4-2.

But the bit in the middle, the actual football? Hmm. No great shakes. Not enough interplay between forwards, not enough touches in the box, not enough penetration with the ball and until the third-placed game the same number of shots on target as Saudi Arabia, who went out after three matches. Croatia exposed the system with their superb wingers and canny striker, pinning England at the back and forcing Southgate's full-backs to defend, meaning England were 5-3-2 with only three in the middle v Croatia's five (the Croat full-backs having pushed up).

Tactically, when all this was going on and the flow of the match started running ever more strongly against England, Southgate didn't change anything. The old football of fear that we've seen in so many England tournament exits came back. A few stats: Kane lost the ball 21 times. Raheem Sterling completed just nine passes. Jordan Pickford kicked the ball long 40 times. Almost half of Henderson's forward passes were unsuccessful. Between them, Ashley Young and Kieran Trippier mustered one successful cross.

So, the bit round the edges was excellent and the guy front-of-house talked a charmingly good game. The nation believed and was able to actually enjoy a tournament again. But that great big bit in the middle, the actual football, still has to get a lot, lot better if England are to make inroads at Euro 2020, where France will be a little older and even better than they were here.

Russia

A revelation to the end. This morning I went up to the Fan Fest on Vorobyovy Hill, overlooking the Luzhniki. In sunshine Moscow stretched out below: hectic, vibrant, exciting and so far from the hellish hive of bureaucracy and spies the propaganda (and our security briefings) said it was. People were nice, people were smiling, people were going about their business and the World Cup was over ... so those claims that these last five weeks were just Putin putting on a show remain hard to believe. If so, he somehow got 300m people to pretend to be the same thing: good, normal, lively, friendly people, not at all different to us. Not even a dictator could choreograph that.

Another Russia story. One of the journalists, who is black, was in outpost Samara, in the middle of a housing estate. He went to a slightly scary-seeming shop on the estate. This guy was eyeballing him. He tried keeping himself to himself but as he walked down one of the aisles he had a tap on the shoulder. Oh, he thought. Here goes. The guy mouthed something he didn't understand. The shopkeeper looked at them. "He is asking if you need any help finding what you want," the shopkeeper said.

Of course there are different stories. Another journalist was mugged in Moscow. His taxi driver seemed a bit strange and wouldn't drop him where he wanted; instead he left him in a dubious area a couple of km from his hotel. He started walking and was almost immediately jumped by two men who pinned him to the ground and stole his phones. He thinks it was a set-up.

There was a moment at the end of the World Cup final that reminded you that, however lovely Russia has been, however nice the people are, to not get too dreamy about it all. It was when the players had to wait for 20 minutes on the pitch for the presentation as Putin and his entourage, and all his security guys, made it down from the VIP seats. That reminded you who is boss, who was throwing the party. And then when Putin, Macron and the Croatian leader, Kolinda Grabar-Kitarovic, were on the podium and torrential rain began falling, there was only one umbrella and it was not chivalrously raised above Mrs Grabar-Kitarovic's head, but Vlad's.

The World Cup
Jonathan Liew, who Gary Lineker not-entirely-hyperbolically calls 'The Messi of Football Reporting', had this to say today: "Even at the very vortex of FIFA's black hole of bullshit remains, perhaps, a kernel of unquestionable truth. Football does bring people together. Football does awaken our collective spirit like nothing else on earth. And in a troubled world, as long as there is a ball and a field and people to play and watch, the reservoir of human happiness will never quite run dry. It's only football. But when it's done right, what a gift it is." As Nigeria found, sometimes you have to bow to Messi. I'm not going to put it any better than that.

France
I was watching them on the pitch, Adel Rami and Samuel Umtiti charging round the perimeter with tricolour flags, Paul Pogba and Blaise Matuidi body surfing across the wet grass through golden ticker tape, Olivier Giroud and Hugo Lloris watching the big screen and laughing about

Lloris' mistake, Benjamin Mendy leading coaching staff on a goofy dance, Antoine Griezmann doing his post-match interviews, little Kante beaming ear to ear in his own, quiet, self-contained space, and I thought: 'Yes, they deserved it.' They are every bit as young and fresh, as multicultural and modern, as eager and unified, as good a good news story as England ever were.

They have the potential to become a great side. They should already be European champions and while they did not always romance us, their football was ruthless, efficient and, on the counter-attack, especially when Mbappe opened up the gears, exhilarating at times. Pour L'Eternite was the headline on the front page of *L'Equipe*, that a fan behind their goal was holding up. Fair play Didier Deschamps – I had really doubted him. Fair play Les Bleus.

Two other thoughts: my, Croatia were good, my they were unlucky in a way. I felt the penalty was a penalty (sorry, but he moved his hand towards the ball – a ref will always give that as a pen, he cannot tell intentionality, he just has to go with the action). But I didn't think the free-kick from which France scored their first was a free-kick and in a first half where Modric, Perisic, Rakitic, Mandzukic and Brozovic were sensational, France without doing much somehow went in 2-1 up. I was moved by Croatia's small-nation pride (as a small-nationer myself) and by their fabulous fans. Modric, a deserved player of the tournament.

Other thought: there is a 'Big Five' in Europe. The Big Five leagues, the football powers. They are Italy, Spain, Germany, France, England. The last four winners of the World Cup have been Italy, Spain, Germany, France ... and England still seem far away. England are still punching well below their weight.

Me: So, in Russia, I have...

- Spent 35 days
- Seen ten games live
- Eaten in 2 Uzbek restaurants
- Checked into eight hotels
- Gained 6lbs
- Written around 60,000 words
- Flown 11,200 miles
- Witnessed, live, 34 goals
- Drank five berry cocktails from a brown paper bag
- Lost to the bridges more times than I beat them

Those words: The majority have been for this blog. I didn't plan to spend so much time on it, but I did it because of you. You who have been reading it. The feedback has been lovely, humbling, exciting. That's what you write for. Thank you so much. I don't know if I'll ever do something like this again, but I do know that it was more than worth it.

So, as they say in Russia …

Do Svidaniya

Until we meet again.

EPILOGUE

No more than six weeks have passed since England met Croatia in that World Cup semi-final at the Luzhniki but football lives in dog years and those 42 days stretch back from now to what seems like a different epoch, a nostalgic age. In this game of ours narratives move so fast that 90 minutes previously can seem another country. Six weeks? A different planet. Albeit there somehow hasn't been enough time for me to get my (now dangerously overdue) Russia expenses done.

The start of a new season has a particular way of making the recent past feel like forever ago. N'Golo Kante gave a rare interview after Chelsea's first game and said: "We all start from zero again, and that's the way our job is. Whatever you did before is quickly forgotten. We all have to go again and prove we are worthy." Not for the first time, from Kante, an impeccable reading of the game.

So, Kante may have left Moscow on July 15 a world champion and the planet's best defensive midfielder, but by August 11 and Chelsea's opening match of the 2018-19 campaign, he found himself recast in a new position – an attacking No.8 – and with the task of winning over his club's new manager, Maurizio Sarri. Typically, without complaint, but with gusto and football intelligence, Kante has been meeting the challenge.

For others it has been more painful turning the page. My last image of Paul Pogba in Russia was of him doing goofy Klinsmann dives across the soaking turf of the Luzhniki into golden shards of ticker tape, as France celebrated winning the World Cup. Today he's on every paper's back page, castigated for his performance v Brighton, at daggers with Jose Mourinho and Ed Woodward. Just two club games in, all that *joie de vivre* sucked out of him already by being re-acquainted with Manchester United's ongoing post-Fergie toil.

At least Pogba is playing. It doesn't matter that Jesse Lingard was a starter in a team that were 22 minutes from the World Cup final – now he is back on Mourinho's bench. Jordan Henderson started the season on Liverpool's. So far, Ruben Loftus-Cheek has not even made Chelsea's and Sarri is offering little encouragement to the belief that his prospects will change.

One of the things I'll most remember about Leicester winning the title was the aftermath. Within a few days of 2015-16 ending, the back pages, phone-ins, the general football conversation, had reverted right back to the norm. Everything was about the giants of the Premier League again. Man U, Man City, Liverpool, Chelsea, Arsenal – who were they signing, who were they hiring?

It was as if anything outside of that regular, familiar narrative – even a 5000-1 fairytale – could only win so much space in people's heads. They returned to the default as quickly as they could. I wonder if it will be the same with the World Cup? What a brilliant summer it was. But as Grandaddy sang: Summer, it's gone.

I spoke to one of the FA's press team today. They deserve medals for how they improved England's press relations in Russia, but they know they're starting from zero, too. Tomorrow the media itinerary for England's first 2018-19 games, v Spain and Switzerland, will be out (the FA first release it via a closed Twitter group – I always forget to check). Today's chat was about being low-key, not wanting to overplay the achievements in Russia, leaving Gareth and staff to quietly get back to business, and so forth. I'd called with an interview idea, but it will have to wait.

I get it, of course I get it. Shame though. From a darts open to closed doors. It will be telling what space we all get to build up the game: usually *The Sunday Times* doesn't go too big on friendlies and next weekend, when any preview pieces will be done, there are also United, Spurs, Arsenal and Old Firm matches to build up. I suspect any lasting 'World Cup effect' will be minimal when it comes to coverage.

What I'm confident of, however, is that when the actual games come round there will be quite a different vibe – in the stadiums and the coverage – compared to England's bland autumn matches a year ago. Being back in Leicester has allowed me to get some sense of the World Cup fever people caught at home. It's not like I've walked in Highcross through a sudden sea of waistcoats, but I found my next-door neighbour on one side got so emotional watching England in Russia he had to keep leaving the room, while the fella on the other side spent most of the summer at his mate's, who built an outdoor bar in his garden to watch the games. Everyone wants to know how the World Cup was and what Russia was like. Their eyes don't glaze over – well not entirely – when you start waxing about the nightlife in Nizhny Novgorod, or Kaliningrad's lakeside culture. They're interested. England are playing in Leicester and our six-year-old is desperate to go to the match. She was moderately into football before, but the World Cup may prove the gateway to making her a proper fan.

And isn't that the lasting power of tournaments? Those league seasons and mega-clubs dominate our agendas. But World Cups (and to a lesser extent Euros, African Nations and Copas, depending on your continent) have the capacity to change them. You can go to a year of gigs but they won't beat a great music festival. Club football splits us, World Cups unite us and thereby shape us. They are our parties, our milestones, our Hogmanays: the marker posts and mountain tops in our lifetime journeys through the game.

We all have a favourite World Cup, and a World Cup that evokes a special time in our lives. Many of us can think of a particular tournament that ignited or reignited our passion for football. Do people have favourite club seasons or "that league campaign which changed my life" in quite the same fashion? Ishbel's 2018 World Cup was my 1978 World Cup. She can keep Harry Kane by the way – I had Archie Gemmill.

We went to France on holiday and spent a couple of weeks at a Eurocamping place and in the bar there was a big screen playing France 4 Croatia 2 on a loop. Bravo the French, their summer in Russia will never be gone. They'll make those memories last, and they also had 1998, and 2000 and 1984. And Henry, Zidane, Platini, Mbappe, Cantona, Vieira and Kante. That's real magic. That's what sustained excellence looks like. That's a true powerhouse nation. And this is the perspective that England should keep. Russia can prove a rebirth, but there's still a lot of growing up to do. Long years of development lie ahead to become a peer of the modern heavyweight international teams like France.

To 2018-19 then: unpacking on July 17, having landed at Heathrow and crawled wearily up the M40 and M69 to Leicester late the night before, I found something in my washbag. It was the plastic hundred-rouble bill that the young, rap-loving Lada taxi driver from Nizhny Novgorod gave me. The one I thought I'd lost.

Remember what he told me? "There are no tickets available for this kind of journey. This is not signified currency but a souvenir. Please accept. It can be your memory." I'm glad to see it again. It's in the flower pot in my office, with my accreditation badge and the phone the company gave me for Russia, and that daft note takes me back.

Jonathan Northcroft
Leicester
August 22, 2018

ACKNOWLEDGEMENTS

DARTS WITH DELE started life as a blog called *Back of the Nyet*, which I began on my journalist Facebook page. The desire to keep producing daily entries, despite a hectic work and travel schedule in Russia, stemmed from the feedback of those who read it. People posted comments that were eclectic, insightful, humbling, leftfield, funny, and went easy on me when my efforts at predicting scores proved pathetic. To an old bloke who filed copy using acoustic couplers and talked via a mobile the size of Artem Dzyuba at his first World Cup, the immediacy and interactivity of digital journalism still feels like a modern wonder.

So, thank you to the following – your feedback on the page was my fuel: Matt Webb, Alec Ross, Chris Pajak, Steve Bennett, Ivan Potapov, Vishnu Charri, Jim Cavanagh, Andrew Pearl, Simon Feilberg, Michael von Herff, Julia Quets, Christopher Altree, Nigel Vause, Michael Flaherty, Alison Meehan, Gary Horgan, Paul Tomkins, Michael Tremarco, Bill Baker, Jimmy Webster, Mike Nevin, Linda Musker, Rupert Wakefield, Michael Flynn, Ron McKay, Gareth Stringer, Dave Harrison, Gavin Price, Duncan Castles, Gary Ward, Rebecca Quinn, Jamie Bowman, Chris Durkin, Julia Ponsford, Scott Burnett, Adam Longley, Julie Sinclair, Miller Fitzgerald, Giles Buckingham, Gordon Henderson, Sean Japp, Maureen Fitzpatrick, Murray Schofield, Tim Gray, Ben Moore, Julian Wakefield, Mark Jacobson, Lee Marlow, Ted Williams, Harry Johnson, Eric McNeil, Kavin Taylor, David Lea, Chris Jones, Andrew Milburn, Mario Humphreys, Larue S'depeche, Judith Hill, Lorne Weeks, Steven Herbert, Peter Fairbrother, Buriel Motlhanka, Debra Bee, Conor Keogh, Alistair Gossip, Jason Hartley, Simon Hart, Stewart Dallas, Graham Ritchie,

Graham Mockford, Malcolm Norquoy, Paul KO, Stephen Rankine, Kenny Hemphill, Richard Wheat, Lee Bailey, Michael O'Neill, Jamie Delaney, Neil Darling, Robin Brown, Michael Walker, Sean Cummins, Ben Rispin, Paul James, Gags Tandon, Matt Davis, Gareth Wall, Stuart Frame, Colin Simpson, Rich White, Simon Pickering, Anthony Mills, Andy Zimmermann, Ian Fulton, Gill Wyness, Ian Briggs, Adam Irwin, Dan Beighton, Martin Tinkler, Danny James, Ross Harte, Keith Quinn, Michael Nemeth, Swarnendu Roy, Tom Challinor, Ste Moore, Matt Powenall, Alasdair McGarry, Ann-Maree Stephen and Ronnie Smith.

One of the subjects I most enjoyed writing about is the camaraderie between journalists: especially when on the road. Thanks to Rob Draper, Mike McGrath, Paul Hetherington, Steve Bates, Simon Mullock, David Walsh, Jason Burt, Matt Dickinson, Neil Ashton, Darren Lewis, Ollie Holt, Michael Church, Shintaro Kano – and many others in the 'pack' – for those little moments that made my trip. Also to Mike and Ethan Tumilty: always great to see your friendly faces when you infiltrate the hacks' battle bus.

Thanks to Rob Sullivan, Greg Demetriou, Andy Walker, James Webb, Jo Plummer, Anna Bush – the FA comms team in Russia. You brought the dartboard, you changed how things were done, you pulled it off. It was easier and better covering England than in any of my tournaments to date. And, for once, no grim 'exit press conference'.

Thank you Matt Needham for the pre World Cup pints, and to Luke, Jim and Ally – the Pontus Kamark Fan Club – for similar. Thanks to Alex, my Russian darts partner in Repino, and the lads from Madani 5-a-sides. I do think playing (however badly) helps a reporter and you're keeping my old legs going. Thank you to Alex Butler, Nick Greenslade, Derek Clements, Greg Struthers, Paul Kenny, Lucy Dupuis – the brilliant office squad on *The Sunday Times*. And to the *Times* desk, particularly Alex Kay-Jelski and Joe Hare – cameos for your World Cup team were an absolute pleasure. Speaking of desks and colleagues, Russia 2018 made me think so much about France 1998, my first World Cup, and Kevin McKenna, Donald Cowey, Graham Spiers, Kevin McCarra and the late Glenn Gibbons. How unbelievably lucky I was to be a young journalist under your collective wings.

Спасибо, spasibo, to Martin Greig and Neil White of BackPage. I always wanted to work with you. Thanks for believing in this. And for being even better at what you do than I thought.

Finally, to mum – dad gets the dedication but you get the eternal thanks. And to Ishbel and Cora, the Ronaldo and Messi of wee girls; and Jan, the Pele of lassies (although I know you'd prefer I said the Dale Gordon). Like a lot else, you made this happen.

Jonathan Northcroft

ABOUT THE AUTHOR

Jonathan Northcroft is the football correspondent of *The Sunday Times* and author of *Fearless: The Amazing Underdog Story of Leicester City, the Greatest Miracle in Sports History*. He has covered every World Cup since 1998 and reports extensively on the English national team.

Facebook and Twitter: @JNorthcroft

BACKPAGE

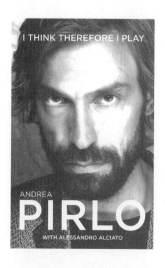

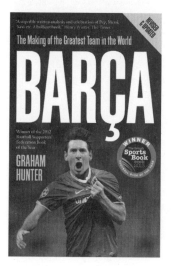

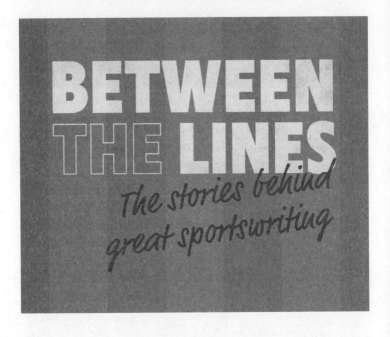

Listen to **'Between the Lines'** podcast.
Search 'Between the Lines' on your podcast
app and click on green logo to subscribe

BackPage interview the biggest names in
sports writing, telling the stories behind
the most memorable books, news stories
and long-form journalism

Episodes include interviews with Jonathan
Northcroft, David Winner, Simon Kuper,
Rory Smith, Grant Wahl, Henry Winter
and many more